PANORAMA

A Selection of Poems
(Revised edition, 1986)

Selected by
J. W. PETERSON

Edited by
A. E. T. BARROW
and
J. FUSTE

W0235347

OXFORD
UNIVERSITY PRESS

OXFORD
UNIVERSITY PRESS

Oxford University Press is a department of the University of Oxford.
It furthers the University's objective of excellence in research, scholarship,
and education by publishing worldwide. Oxford is a registered trade mark of
Oxford University Press in the UK and in certain other countries.

Published in India by
Oxford University Press
22 Workspace, 2nd Floor, 1/22 Asaf Ali Road, New Delhi 110002

ISBN-13: 978-0-19-562031-3
ISBN-10: 0-19-562031-3

Printed in India by Repro India Ltd.

For product information and current price, please visit www.india.oup.com

Third-party website addresses mentioned in this book are provided
by Oxford University Press in good faith and for information only.
Oxford University Press disclaims any responsibility for the material
contained therein.

CONTENTS

1. Nature

William Blake	*The Echoing Green*	1
William Wordsworth	*To a Skylark*	2
H.L.V. Derozio	*Night*	2
W.B. Yeats	*The Lake Isle of Innisfree*	5
P.B. Shelley	*To a Skylark*	5
John Keats	*Ode to a Nightingale*	9
John Masefield	*The West Wind*	11
Joseph Furtado	*The Cornfield*	12
A.K. Ramanujan	*A River*	14

2. Reflection

William Shakespeare	*The Bees*	16
Sir Henry Wotton	*Character of a Happy Life*	16
George Herbert	*The Pulley*	17
William Cowper	*Light Shining out of Darkness*	18
William Blake	*The Tiger*	19
William Wordsworth	*Sleep*	19
Thomas Hardy	*The Darkling Thrush*	20
Christina Rossetti	*Uphill*	21
Patrick Fernando	*Ballad of a River*	21

3. Sorrow

John Milton	*On his Blindness*	23
Nissim Ezekiel	*Night of the Scorpion*	23

William Wordsworth	*Written in London,*	
	September 1802	25
John Keats	*When I have Fears*	25
Robert Frost	*Stopping by Woods*	
	on a Snowy Evening	26
Wilfred Owen	*Futility*	26
Patrick Fernando	*The Fisherman*	
	Mourned by his Wife	27
Jayanta Mahapatra	*The Captive Air of*	
	Chandipur-on-Sea	28

4. Men and Women

William Shakespeare	*Seven Ages of Man*	29
H.W. Longfellow	*The Village Blacksmith*	30
Oliver Goldsmith	*The Village Schoolmaster*	31
William Wordsworth	*The Solitary Reaper*	32
Sir Thomas Campbell	*Lord Ullin's Daughter*	33
Robert Southey	*The Scholar*	35
James Leigh Hunt	*Abou Ben Adhem*	35
R.L. Stevenson	*The Vagabond*	36
Toru Dutt	*Sita*	37

5. Love

John Donne	*The Sun Rising*	39
Robert Herrick	*The Night Piece: To Julia*	40
Robert Burns	*John Anderson My Jo*	40
Lord Byron	*She Walks in Beauty*	41
Thomas Moore	*Believe Me, if all those*	
	Endearing Young Charms	41
H.W. Longfellow	*Hiawatha's Wooing*	42
P.B. Shelley	*Lines to an Indian Air*	50

Hartley Coleridge	*She is not Fair to Outward View*	51
Kamala Das	*My Grandmother's House*	51

6. Ballads and Narratives

Sir Walter Scott	*Lochinvar*	52
A.K. Ramanujan	*A Minor Sacrifice*	53
Robert Southey	*The Inchcape Rock*	58
H.W. Longfellow	*The Slave's Dream*	60
Robert Browning	*The Pied Piper of Hamelin*	62
Rudyard Kipling	*The Ballad of East and West*	70
Alfred Noyes	*The Highwayman*	74
Armando Menezes	*The Train*	78
Lord Macaulay	*Horatius*	79

7. Patriotism

H.L.V. Derozio	*To India—My Native Land*	87
S.C. Dutt	*The Warrior's Return*	87
Rabindranath Tagore	*Where the Mind is Without Fear*	89
Nissim Ezekiel	*The Patriot*	90
Sir Walter Scott	*Patriotism*	91
Robert Browning	*The Patriot*	92
Sir Henry Newbolt	*Ireland, Ireland*	93
W.B. Yeats	*Easter 1916*	93
Rupert Brooke	*The Soldier*	96

8. Death and Heroism

James Shirley	*Death the Leveller*	97
Samuel Johnson	*On the Death of Mr Robert Levet A Practiser in Physic*	98
Lord Byron	*The Dying Gladiator*	99
Lord Tennyson	*From 'The Passing of Arthur'*	100
W.B. Yeats	*An Irish Airman foresees his Death*	105
H.C. Dutt	*Aurungzeb at his Father's Bier*	106
Gieve Patel	*On Killing a Tree*	108
Walt Whitman	*O Captain! My Captain!*	109

9. Historical Characters, Scenes and Events

A.K. Ramanujan	*Some Indian uses of History on a Rainy Day*	110
Robert Southey	*After Blenheim*	111
Charles Wolfe	*The Burial of Sir John Moore at Corunna*	113
H.W. Longfellow	*Paul Revere's Ride*	115
W.M. Thackeray	*King Canute*	118
Michael Madhusudan Dutt	*King Porus—A Legend of Old*	120
Lord Tennyson	*Ulysses*	124
William Wordsworth	*Upon Westminster Bridge September 3, 1802*	126
Lord Byron	*Sonnet on Chillon*	127

10. Satire and Humour

William Cowper	*John Gilpin*	128
W.H. Auden	*Miss Gee*	136
John Dryden	*Zimri: The Duke of*	
	Buckingham	139
T.S. Eliot	*Macavity: The*	
	Mystery Cat	140
Nissim Ezekiel	*The Professor*	142
Lewis Carroll	*The Walrus and the*	
	Carpenter	143
D.H. Lawrence	*Mosquito*	146
Ian Crichton Smith	*The Nose*	149
Ashok Mahajan	*Culture*	150

ACKNOWLEDGEMENTS

To the Tagore Estate and Macmillan Co. of India Ltd for 'Where the mind is without fear' by Rabindranath Tagore; to Philip Furtado for 'The Cornfield' by Joseph Furtado; to the poet for 'The Train' by Armando Menezes; to the poet for 'Night of the Scorpion', 'The Patriot', and 'The Professor' by Nissim Ezekiel; to the poet for 'My Grandmother's House' by Kamala Das; to the poet for 'On Killing a Tree' by Gieve Patel; to the Society of Authors and Jonathan Cape Ltd for 'Loveliest of Trees' by A. E. Housman; to M. B. Yeats, Miss Anne Yeats and Macmillan of London & Basingstoke for 'Easter 1916' and 'An Irish Airman foresees his Death' by W. B. Yeats; to Mrs George Bambridge and Eyre Methuen Ltd for 'The Ballad of East and West' from Complete Barrack Room Ballads by Rudyard Kipling; to the Society of Authors for "The West Wind' by John Masefield; to the estate of Robert Frost, Edward Connery Latham (editor) and Jonathan Cape Ltd for 'Stopping By Woods on a Snowy Evening' from The Poetry of Robert Frost; to the poet and John Murray Ltd for 'The Highwayman' by Alfred Noyes from Collected Poems; to Mrs B. G. Fernando for 'The Fisherman Mourned by His Wife' and 'Ballad of a River' by Patrick Fernando; to the poet for 'A River', 'Some Indian uses of History on a Rainy Day' and 'A Minor Sacrifice' by A. K. Ramanujan; to Faber and Faber Ltd for 'Miss Gee' by W. H. Auden and 'The Nose' by Ian Crichton Smith.

1. NATURE

THE ECHOING GREEN

The sun does arise,
And make happy the skies;
The merry bells ring
To welcome the Spring;
The sky-lark and thrush,
The birds of the bush,
Sing louder around
To the bells' cheerful sound,
While our sports shall be seen
On the Echoing Green.

Old John, with white hair,
Does laugh away care.
Sitting under the oak,
Among the old folk.
They laugh at our play,
And soon they all say:
'Such, such were the joys
When we all, girls and boys.
In our youth-time were seen
On the Echoing Green'

Till the little ones, weary,
No more can be merry;
The sun does descend,
And our sports have an end.
Round the laps of their mothers
Many sisters and brothers.
Like birds in their nest.
Are ready for rest,
And sport no more seen
On the darkening Green.

WILLIAM BLAKE

TO A SKYLARK

Ethereal minstrel! pilgrim of the sky!
Dost thou despise the earth where cares abound?
Or, while thy wings aspire, are heart and eye
Both with thy nest upon the dewy ground?
Thy nest, which thou canst drop into at will,
Those quivering wings composed, that music still!

To the last point of vision, and beyond,
Mount, daring warbler!—that love-prompted strain
—'Twixt thee and thine a never-failing bond—
Thrills not the less the bosom of the plain:
Yet might'st thou seem, proud privilege! to sing
All independent of the leafy Spring.

Leave to the nightingale her shady wood:
A privacy of glorious light is thine,
Whence thou dost pour upon the world a flood
Of harmony, with instinct more divine;
Type of the wise who soar, but never roam—
True to the kindred points of Heaven and Home!

WILLIAM WORDSWORTH

NIGHT

I

For loneliness and thought this is the hour:—
    Now that thou smil'st so beautiful and bright,
Oh! how I feel thy soul-subduing power,
    And gaze upon thy loveliness, sweet Night!
    There sails the moon, like a small silver bark
    Floating upon the ocean vast and dark:
Lovers should only look upon her light,
    And only by her light should lovers meet;
They catch an inspiration from the sight,

And all their words flow musically sweet.
Like the soft fall of waters far away;
    Their hearts run o'er with gladness, till they seem
As if they were not beings of the day,
    But beautiful creations of a dream!

II

Night, Night, O Night! thou hast a gentle face,
    Like a fond mother's smiling o'er her child!
I gaze on thee till my soul swells apace
    With thoughts, and aspirations, high and wild.
'Tis ever so; and there be some, who find
    That when the eye is fixed on boundless space
Spurning the earth, vast grows the giant mind,
    And seeks in some bright orb a dwelling-place.
And it may be, that in my breast the fires
    Of hope, and fancy both are burning bright;
And all my aspirations, and desires
    May pass away, e'en with thy shadows, Night!
But could my spirit fly from earth afar,
'Twould dwell with one I love in yonder lovely star.

III

Oh! how fond memory in the calm of night
    Brings to the mind young love, though love hath past,
With all th' endearing things which gave delight,
    And which we once believed could always last!
Oft at this hour, in happier days I deem,
    When, Time! thy foot fell softly upon flowers,
And lighted by Diana's purest beam,
    Have youthful hearts enjoyed the passing hours;
And as the lover named the loved-one's name,
    Pale grew her cheek, while glowed the fire within,
Like pure asbestos whitened by the flame;
    Then did the madness of his heart begin;
And then he gazed upon her forehead fair,
Then looked into her eyes, to see if love was there.

IV

Swift as the dark eye's glance or falcon's flight,
Thought comes on thought, awakened by the night—
And there are some which point towards the past,
   And fondly linger o'er life's twilight sky,
   Hailing the sacred star of memory;
And thou, though lonely, thou, my poor heart, hast
Much to muse over of past happiness,
And though 'tis gone for ever, not the less
Is its remembrance dear:—but lo! a cloud
Hath wrapt the moon, like beauty in a shroud!
Hush! there is silence—but methinks mine ear
A distant, sweet, seraphic hymn doth hear—
The stars alone are watching from above.
Hush! 'tis the night wind's voice—ah! soft as hers I love.

V

This to the soul of feeling sadness brings,
   And painful thoughts of those who once were dear,
   But who, now far from bleak misfortune's sphere,
Fly on from world to world with golden wings;
   This wakes in many an eye a hopeless tear;
'Tis vainly shed, for still the fond heart clings
   (Though sorrow all its best enjoyments sear)
Unto the memory of vanished things!—
The moon is gone; and thus go those we love;
   The night winds wail; and thus for them we mourn.
The stars look down; thus spirits from above
   Hallow the mourner's tears upon the urn.
Some thoughts are all of joy, and some of woe;
Mine end in tears—they're welcome—let them flow.

VI

Ye tears that flow, ye sighs that break the heart,
Ah! wherefore do ye not relieve the wound,
The deadly wound which Griefs envenomed dart
   Gives to the breast whose blood must stream unbound?

Ah! no, it must not be!—tears wildly start,
And sighs are heaved, and blood sinks in the ground;
　But these bring no relief:—we look around,
But vainly look for those who formed a part
　Of us, as we of them, and whom we wore
　Like gems in bezils, in the heart's deep core.
Where are they now?—gone to that 'narrow cell'
Whose gloom no lamp hath broken, nor shall break,
Whose secrets never spirit came to tell:—
O! that their day might dawn, for then they would awake.

HENRY LOUIS VIVIAN DEROZIO

THE LAKE ISLE OF INNISFREE

I will arise and go now, and go to Innisfree,
And a small cabin build there, of clay and wattles made:
Nine bean-rows will I have there, a hive for the honey-bee,
And live alone in the bee-loud glade.

And I shall have some peace there, for peace comes dropping
　slow,
Dropping from the veils of the morning to where the cricket sings;
There midnight's all a glimmer, and noon a purple glow,
And evening full of the linnet's wings.

I will arise and go now, for always night and day
I hear lake water lapping with low sounds by the shore;
While I stand on the roadway, or on the pavements grey,
I hear it in the deep heart's

W.B. YEATS

TO A SKYLARK

Hail to thee, blithe spirit!
　Bird thou never wert,
That from heaven, or near it.
　Pourest thy full heart
In profuse strains of unpremeditated art.

Higher still and higher
From the earth thou springest
Like a cloud of fire;
The blue deep thou wingest,
And singing still dost soar, and soaring ever singest

In the golden lightning
Of the sunken sun,
O'er which clouds are brightening
Thou dost float and run,
Like an unbodied joy whose race is just begun.

The pale purple even
Melts around thy flight
Like a star of heaven
In the broad daylight
Thou art unseen, but yet I hear thy shrill delight—

Keen as are the arrows
Of that silver sphere
Whose intense lamp narrows
In the white dawn clear,
Until we hardly see, we feel that it is there.

All the earth and air
With thy voice is loud
As, when night is bare,
From one lonely cloud
The moon rains out her beams, and heaven is overflow'd.

What thou art we know not;
What is most like thee?
From rainbow clouds there flow not
Drops so bright to see
As from thy presence showers a rain of melody.

Like a poet hidden
    In the light of thought,
Singing hymns unbidden,
    Till the world is wrought
To sympathy with hopes and fears it heeded not:

Like a high-born maiden
    In a palace tower,
Soothing her love-laden
    Soul in secret hour
With music sweet as love, which overflows her bower:

Like a glow-worm golden
    In a dell of dew,
Scattering unbeholden
    Its aerial hue
Among the flowers and grass, which screen it from the view:

Like a rose embower'd
    In its own green leaves,
By warm winds deflower'd,
    Till the scent it gives
Makes faint with too much sweet these heavy-winged thieves:

Sound of vernal showers
    On the twinkling grass,
Rain-awaken'd flowers—
    All that ever was
Joyous and clear and fresh—thy music doth surpass.

Teach us, sprite or bird,
    What sweet thoughts are thine:
I have never heard
    Praise of love or wine
That panted forth a flood of rapture so divine

Chorus hymeneal,
 Or triumphal chant,
Match'd With thine would be all
 But an empty vaunt—
A thing wherein we feel there is some hidden want.

What objects are the fountains
 Of thy happy strain?
What fields, or waves, or mountains?
 What shapes of sky or plain?
What love of thine own kind? What ignorance of pain?

With thy clear keen joyance
 Languor cannot be:
Shadow of annoyance
 Never came near thee:
Thou lovest, but ne'er knew love's sad satiety.

Waking or asleep
 Thou of death must deem
Things more true and deep
 Than we mortals dream,
Or how could thy notes flow in such a crystal stream?

We look before and after,
 And pine for what is not:
Our sincerest laughter
 With some pain is fraught;
Our sweetest songs are those that tell of saddest thought.

Yet if we could scorn
 Hate, and pride, and fear;
If we were things born
 Not to shed a tear,
I know not how thy joy we ever should come near.

Better than all measures
Of delightful sound,
Better than all treasures
That in books are found,
Thy skill to poet were, thou scorner of the ground!

Teach me half the gladness
That thy brain must know,
Such harmonious madness
From my lips would flow,
The world should listen then, as I am listening now!

Percy Bysshe Shelley

ODE TO A NIGHTINGALE

My heart aches, and a drowsy numbness pains
My sense, as though of hemlock I had drunk,
Or emptied some dull opiate to the drains
One minute past, and Lethe-wards had sunk:
'Tis not through envy of thy happy lot,
But being too happy in thy happiness,
That thou, light-winged Dryad of the trees,
In some melodious plot
Of beechen green, and shadows numberless,
Singest of summer in full-throated ease.

O for a draught of vintage! that hath been
Cooled a long age in the deep-delved earth,
Tasting of Flora and the country green,
Dance, and Provencal song, and sunburnt mirth!
O for a beaker full of the warm South!
Full of the true, the blushful Hippocrene,
With beaded bubbles winking at the brim,
And purple-stained mouth
That I might drink, and leave the world unseen,
And with thee fade away into the forest dim:

Fade far away, dissolve, and quite forget
    What thou among the leaves hast never known,
The weariness, the fever, and the fret
    Here, where men sit and hear each other groan;
Where palsy shakes a few, sad, last grey hairs,
    Where youth grows pale, and spectre-thin, and dies;
        Where but to think is to be full of sorrow
            And leaden-eyed despairs;
    Where Beauty cannot keep her lustrous eyes,
        Or new Love pine at them beyond to-morrow

Away! away! for 1 will fly to thee,
    Not charioted by Bacchus and his pards,
But on the viewless wings of Poesy,
    Though the dull brain perplexes and retards:
Already with thee! tender is the night,
    And happy the Queen-Moon is on her throne,

        Cluster'd around by all her starry Fays;
            But here there is no light,
    Save what from heaven is with the breezes blown
        Through verdurous glooms and winding mossy ways.

I cannot see what flowers are at my feet,
    Nor what soft incense hangs upon the boughs,
But, in embalmed darkness, guess each sweet
    Wherewith the seasonable month endows
The grass, the thicket, and the fruit-tree wild;
    White hawthorn, and the pastoral eglantine;
        Fast fading violets cover'd up in leaves;
            And mid-May's eldest child,
    The coming musk-rose, full of dewy wine,
        The murmurous haunt of flies on summer eves.

Darkling I listen; and for many a time
    I have been half in love with easeful Death,
Called him soft names in many a mused rhyme,
    To take into the air my quiet breath;
Now more than ever seems it rich to die,
    To cease upon the midnight with no pain,

While thou art pouring forth thy soul abroad

In such an ecstasy!
Still wouldst thou sing, and I have ears in vain—
To thy high requiem become a sod.

Thou was not born for death, immortal Bird'
No hungry generations tread thee clown;
The voice I hear this passing night was heard
In ancient days by emperor and clown:
Perhaps the self-same song that found a path
Through the sad heart of Ruth, when, sick for home,
She stood in tears amid the alien corn;

The same that oft-times hath
Charm'd magic casements, opening on the foam
Of perilous seas, in faery lands forlorn.
Forlorn! the very word is like a bell
To toll me back from thee to my sole self!
Adieu! the fancy cannot cheat so well
As she is famed to do, deceiving elf.
Adieu! adieu! thy plaintive anthem fades
Past the near meadows, over the still stream,
Up the hill-side; and now 'tis buried deep
In the next valley-glades:
Was it a vision, or a waking dream!
Fled is that music:—do I wake or sleep?

JOHN KEATS

THE WEST WIND

It's a warm wind, the west wind, full of birds' cries;
I never hear the west wind but tears are in my eyes,
For it comes from the west lands, the old brown hills,
And April's in the west wind, and daffodils.

It's a fine land, the west land, for hearts as tired as mine,
Apple orchards blossom there, and the air's like wine.
There is cool green grass there, where men may lie at rest,

And the thrushes are in song there, fluting from the nest.

'Will ye not come home, brother? Ye have been long away:
It's April, and blossom time, and white is the May;
And bright is the sun, brother, and warm is the rain,—
Will ye not come home, brother, home to us again?

'The young corn is green, brother, where the rabbits run,
It's blue sky, and white clouds, and warm rain and sun.
It's song to a man's soul, brother, fire to a man's brain,
To hear the wild bees and see the merry spring again.

'Larks are singing in the west, brother, above the green wheat,
So will ye not come home, brother, and rest your tired feet?
I've a balm for bruised hearts, brother, sleep for aching eyes,
Says the warm wind, the west wind, full of birds' cries.
It's the white road westwards is the road I must tread
To the green grass, the cool grass, and rest for heart and head
To the violets and the warm hearts and the thrushes' song,
In the fine land, the west land, the land where I belong.

JOHN MASEFIELD

THE CORNFIELD

One autumn morn
I chanced to cross
A field of corn;
And there it was—
That blessed morn—.
To sintul me
The grace was given
On earth to see
The ways of Heaven:
1 saw a bird
And heard a voice
I ne'er before
Had seen or heard.
I did rejoice,

Yet with my joy
Was holy awe
At what I saw;
And what I said
I know not well,
For, strange to tell,
I instantly
Was on my knee.

The bird saw too.
Yet did not stir;
And, 'Who are you
To ask me, sir?'.
It said, and I
Did thus reply.
Grown bolder now,
I know not how:
'An untaught poet
Of trees and birds
Whom no man knoweth
And, wanting words,
But dreams and sings
Of simple things.'—
'Peace! all heaven knoweth;
From heaven come I:
Come, simple poet,'
The bird rejoined.

So I drew nigh
And heard it say—
That blessed day—
To an ear of corn,
A tiny ear
'Grow, quick, my dear!
There's dearth and death
On every hand,
In every breath
Upon this land—
Grow quick, my dear!'

Then was revealed
At every ear,
Throughout the field,
A bird, and clear
A voice, 'Spare, spare!'
Was it my prayer
That blessed morn
While I did cross
The field of corn?
Perchance it was:
To sinful me
Such grace was given—
On earth to see
The ways of Heaven.

JOSEPH FURTADO

A RIVER

In Madurai,
　　　　　　city of temples and poets
who sang of cities and temples:
every summer
a river dries to a trickle
in the sand,
baring the sand-ribs,
straw and women's hair
clogging the Watergates
at the rusty bars
under the bridges with patches
of repair all over them
the wet stones glistening like sleepy
crocodiles, the dry ones
shaven water-buffaloes lounging in the sun.
The poets sang only of the floods.

He was there for a day

when they had the floods.
People everywhere talked
of the inches rising,
of the precise number of cobbled steps
run over by the water, rising
on the bathing places,
and the way it carried off three village houses,
one pregnant woman
and a couple of cows
named Gopi and Brinda as usual.

The new poets still quoted
the old poets, but no one spoke
in verse
of the pregnant woman
drowned, with perhaps twins in her,
kicking at blank walls
even before birth.
He said:
the river has water enough
to be poetic
about only once a year
and then
it carries away
in the first half-hour
three village houses,
a couple of cows
named Gopi and Brinda
and one pregnant woman
expecting identical twins
with no moles on their bodies,
with different–coloured diapers

to tell them apart.

A. K. RAMANUJAN

2. REFLECTION

THE BEES

        So work the honey-bees,
Creatures that by a rule in nature teach
The act of order to a peopled kingdom.
They have a king, and officers of sorts;
Where some, like magistrates, correct at home;
Others, like merchants, venture trade abroad;
Others, like soldiers, armed in their stings,
Make boot upon the summer's velvet buds;
Which pillage they with merry march bring home
To the tent royal of their emperor;
Who, busied in his majesty, surveys,
The singing masons building roofs of gold,
The civil citizens kneading up the honey,
The poor mechanic porters crowding in
Their heavy burdens at his narrow gate,
The sad-eyed justice, with his surly hum,
Delivering o'er to executors pale
The lazy yawning drone.

      WILLIAM SHAKESPEARE (*Henry V*)

CHARACTER OF A HAPPY LIFE

How happy is he born or taught
   That serveth not another's will;
Whose armour is his honest thought,
   And simple truth his utmost skill!

Whose passions not his masters are,
   Whose soul is still prepared for death;
Untied unto the world with care
   Of princely love or vulgar breath;

Who hath his life from rumours freed,

Whose conscience is his strong retreat;
Whose state can neither flatterers feed,
   Nor ruin make oppressors great;

Who envies none whom chance doth raise
   Nor vice; who never understood
How deepest wounds are given with praise;
   Nor rules of state, but rules of good;

Who God doth late and early pray
   More of his grace than gifts to lend;
Who entertains the harmless day
   With a well-chosen book or friend;

—This man is free from servile bands
   Of hope to rise, or fear to fall;
Lord of himself, though not of lands;
   And having nothing, he hath all.

Sir Henry Wotton

THE PULLEY

   When God at first made man,
Having a glass of blessings standing by,
'Let us', said he, 'pour on him all we can:
Let the world's riches, which dispersed lie,
        Contract into a span'.

   So strength first made a way;
Then beauty flowed, then wisdom, honour, pleasure;
When almost all was out. God made a stay,
Perceiving that, alone of all his treasure,
        Rest in the bottom lay.

   'For if 1 should', said he,
'Bestow this jewel also on my creature,
He would adore my gifts instead of me.
And rest in Nature, not the God of Nature:
        So both should losers be.

'Yet let him keep the rest,
But keep them with repining restlessness;
Let him be rich and weary, that at least,
If goodness lead him not, yet weariness
              May toss him to my breast.

                                        GEORGE HERBERT

LIGHT SHINING OUT OF DARKNESS

God moves in a mysterious way,
    His wonders to perform;
He plants his footsteps in the sea.
    And rides upon the storm.

Deep in unfathomable mines
    Of never failing skill
He treasures up his bright designs,
    And works his sovereign will.

Ye fearful saints, fresh courage take,
    The clouds ye so much dread
Are big with mercy, and shall break
    In blessings on your head.

Judge not the Lord by feeble sense,
    But trust him for his grace;
Behind a frowning providence,
    He hides a smiling face.

His purposes will ripen fast,
    Unfolding every hour;
The bud may have a bitter taste,
    But sweet will be the flower.

Blind unbelief is sure to err,
    And scan his work in vain;
God is his own interpreter,
    And he will make it plain.

                                        WILLIAM COWPER

THE TIGER

Tiger! Tiger! burning bright
In the forests of the night,
What immortal hand or eye
Could frame thy fearful symmetry?

In what distant deeps or skies
Burnt the fire of thine eyes?
On what wings dare he aspire?
What the hand dare seize the fire?

And what shoulder and what art
Could twist the sinews of thy heart?
And, when thy heart began to beat,
What dread hand and what dread feet?

What the hammer? What the chain?
In what furnace was thy brain?
What the anvil? What dread grasp
Dare its deadly terrors clasp?

When the stars threw down their spears,
And water'd heaven with their tears,
Did He smile His work to see?
Did He who made the lamb make thee?

Tiger! Tiger! burning bright
In the forests of the night,
What immortal hand or eye
Dare frame thy fearful symmetry?

WILLIAM BLAKE

SLEEP

A flock of sheep that leisurely pass by
One after one; the sound of rain, and bees
Murmuring; the fall of rivers, winds and seas,
Smooth fields, white sheets of water, and pure sky—
I've thought of all by turns and yet do lie

Sleepless; and soon the small birds' melodies
Must hear first uttered from my orchard trees
And the first cuckoo's melancholy cry
Even thus last night, and two nights more I lay
And could not win thee. Sleep! by any stealth;
So do not let me wear to-night away:
Without thee what is all the morning's wealth?
Come, blessed barrier between day and day,
Dear mother of fresh thoughts and joyous health.

WILLIAM WORDSWORTH

THE DARKLING THRUSH

I leant upon a coppice gate
    When Frost was spectre–gray.
And Winter's dregs made desolate
    The weakening eye of day.
The tangled bine-stems scored the sky
    Like strings of broken lyres,
And all mankind that haunted nigh
    Had sought their household fires.

The land's sharp features seemed to be
    The Century's corpse outleant,
His crypt the cloudy canopy.
    The wind his death-lament.
The ancient pulse of germ and birth
    Was shrunken hard and dry,
And every spirit upon earth
    Seemed fervourless as I.

At once a voice arose among
    The bleak twigs overhead
In a full-hearted evensong
    Of joy illimited;
An aged thrush, frail, gaunt, and small
    In blast-beruffled plume,

Had chosen thus to fling his soul
  Upon the growing gloom.
So little cause for carollings
  Of such ecstatic sound
Was written on terrestrial things
  Afar or nigh around,
That I could think there trembled through
  His happy good-night air
Some blessed Hope, whereof he knew
  And I was unaware.

THOMAS HARDY

UPHILL

Does the road wind uphill all the way?
  Yes, to the very end.
Will the day's journey take the whole long day?
  From morn to night, my friend.

But is there for the night a resting-place?
  A roof for when the slow, dark hours begin.
May not the darkness hide it from my face?
  You cannot miss that inn.

Shall I meet other wayfarers at night?
  Those who have gone before.
Then must I knock, or call when just in sight?
  They will not keep you standing at that door.

Shall I find comfort, travel-sore and weak?
  Of labour you shall find the sum.
Will there be beds for me and all who seek?
  Yea, beds for all who come.

CHRISTINA ROSSETTI

BALLAD OF A RIVER

Dawn fires the surface into gold,
Gold-eyed the herons stilt and stalk.

At silver noon the waters hold
Wheelings of a mirrored hawk.

I've not seen water lie so still
As here. Perhaps an otter may
Disturb its peace, or white cranes till
The green edge wading tall-knee-deep.

In gusts of wind, a faint wood hum—
Plucked leaves and broken petals dance.
The wind departs, the wood is dumb.
And floating yellows gather brown.

To think up to a mile ago
This river bounded like a hound,
Convulsed and nearly wrecked our boat,
And lies here gentle as a pond!

A rich practical man I'm told
Demanded, why this idleness?
He got no answer and compelled
The river into harness

Like frightened birds the minutes fled
Pursued by roaring steel and fire.
The river slaved and profits grew
To almost overtake desire.

Until, they say, one windy night,
In deepest vigils of the owl,
The river rose and foaming white
Descended like a murderer.

At dawn the waters shone restored.
The wreckage stood like blasted rocks
Round which the burnished mirror showed
Artistry of a wild brown hawk.

                              PATRICK FERNANDO

3. SORROW

ON HIS BLINDNESS

When I consider how my light is spent
  Ere half my days, in this dark world and wide,
  And that one talent, which is death to hide,
  Lodged with me useless, though my soul more bent
To serve therewith my Maker, and present
  My true account, lest He, returning, chide;
  'Doth God exact day-labour, light denied?'
  I fondly ask: but Patience, to prevent
That murmur, soon, replies, 'God doth not need
  Either man's work, or His own gifts; who best
  Bear His mild yoke, they serve Him best; His state
Is kingly: thousands at His bidding speed,
  And post o'er land and ocean without rest;
  They also serve who only stand and wait.'

JOHN MILTON

NIGHT OF THE SCORPION

I remember the night my mother
was stung by a scorpion. Ten hours
of steady rain had driven him
to crawl beneath a sack of rice.
Parting with his poison—flash
of diabolic tail in the dark room—
he risked the rain again.
The peasants came like swarms of flies
and buzzed the Name of God a hundred times
to paralyse the Evil One.
With candles and with lanterns
throwing giant scorpion shadows
on the mud-baked walls

they searched for him: he was not found.
They clicked their tongues.
With every movement that the scorpion made
his poison moved in mother's blood, they said.
May he sit still, they said.
May the sins of your previous birth
be burned away tonight, they said.
May your suffering decrease
the misfortunes of your next birth, they said.
May the sum of evil
balanced in this unreal world
against the sum of good
become diminished by your pain
May the poison purify your flesh
of desire, and your spirit of ambition,
they said, and they sat around
on the floor with my mother in the centre,
the peace of understanding on each face.

More candles, more lanterns, more neighbours,
more insects, and the endless rain.
My mother twisted through and through
groaning on a mat.
My father, sceptic, rationalist,
trying every curse and blessing,
powder, mixture, herb and hybrid.
He even poured a little paraffin
upon the bitten toe and put a match to it.
I watched the flame feeding on my mother.
1 watched the holy man perform his rites
to tame the poison with an incantation.
After twenty hours
it lost its sting.

My mother only said
Thank God the scorpion picked on me
and spared my children.

                                          NISSIM EZEKIEL

WRITTEN IN LONDON, SEPTEMBER, 1802

O friend! I know not which way I must look
For comfort, being, as I am, opprest
To think that now our life is only drest
For show; mean handiwork of craftsman, cook,
Or groom!—We must run glittering like a brook
In the open sunshine, or we are unblest;
The wealthiest man among us is the best:
No grandeur now in Nature or in book
Delights us. Rapine, avarice, expense,
This is idolatry; and these we adore:
Plain living and high thinking are no more:
The homely beauty of the good old cause
Is gone; our peace, our fearful innocence,
And pure-religion breathing household laws.

WILLIAM WORDSWORTH

WHEN I HAVE FEARS

When I have fears that I may cease to be
Before my pen has glean'd my teeming brain,
Before high-piled books, in charact'ry,
Hold like rich garners the full-ripen'd grain;
When I behold, upon the night's starr'd face,
Huge cloudy symbols of a high romance,
And think that I may never live to trace
Their shadows, with the magic hand of chance;
And when I feel, fair creature of an hour!
That I shall never look upon thee more,
Never have relish in the faery power
Of unreflecting love—then on the shore
Of the wide world I stand alone, and think,
Till love and fame to nothingness do sink.

JOHN KEATS

STOPPING BY WOODS ON A SNOWY EVENING

Whose woods these are I think I know.
His house is in the village though;
He will not see me stopping here
To watch his woods fill up with snow.

My little horse must think it queer
To stop without a farmhouse near
Between the woods and frozen lake
The darkest evening of the year.

He gives his harness bells a shake
To ask if there is some mistake.
The only other sound's the sweep
Of easy wind and downy flake.

The woods are lovely, dark and deep,
But I have promises to keep,
And miles to go before I sleep,
And miles to go before I sleep.

　　　　　　　　　　　　　　　ROBERT FROST

FUTILITY

Move him into the sun—
Gently its touch awoke him once,
At home, whispering of fields unsown.
Always it woke him, even in France.
Until this morning and this snow.
If anything might rouse him now
The kind old sun will know.

Think how it wakes the seeds,—
Woke, once, the clays of a cold star.
Are limbs, so dear-achieved, are sides.
Full-nerved—still warm—too hard to stir?
Was it far this the clay grew tall.?

—O what made fatuous sunbeams toil
To break earth's sleep at all?

WILFRED OWEN

THE FISHERMAN MOURNED BY HIS WIFE

When you were not quite thirty and the sun
Had not yet tanned you into old-boat brown,
When you were not quite thirty and had not begun
To be embittered like the rest, nor grown
Obsessed with death, then would you come
Hot with continence upon the sea
Chaste as a gull flying pointed home,
In haste to be with me!

Now that, being dead, you are beyond detection,
And I need not be discreet, let us confess
It was not love that married us nor affection,
But elders' persuasion, not even loneliness.
Recall how first you were so impatient and afraid,
My eyes were open in the dark unlike in love,
Trembling, lest in fear, you'll let me go a maid,
Trembling on the other hand, for my virginity.

Three months the monsoon thrashed the sea, and you
Remained at home; the sky cracked like a shell
In thunder, and the rain broke through.
At last when pouring ceased and storm winds fell,
When gulls returned new-plumed and wild,
When in our wind-torn flamboyante
New buds broke. I was with child.

My face was wan while telling you and voice fell low,
And you seemed full of guilt and not to know
Whether to repent or rejoice over the situation.
You nodded at the ground and went to sea.
But soon I was to you more than God or temptation,
And so were you to me.

Men come and go, some say they understand,
Our children weep, the youngest thinks you're fast asleep:

Theirs is fear and wonderment.
You had grown so familiar as my hand.
That I cannot with simple grief
Assuage dismemberment.
Outside the wind despoils of leaf
Trees that it used to nurse;
Once more the flamboyante is torn,
The sky cracks like a shell again,
So someone practical has gone
To make them bring the hearse
Before the rain.

PATRICK FERNANDO

THE CAPTIVE AIR OF CHANDIPUR-ON-SEA

Day after day the drunk sea at Chandipur
spits out the gauze wings of shells along the beach
and rumples the thin air behind the sands.
Who can tell of the songs of this sea that go on
to baffle and double the space around our lives?
Or of smells paralysed through the centuries,
of deltas hard and white that stretched once
to lure the feet of women bidding their men goodbye?
Or of salt and light that dark and provocative eyes
demanded, their shoulders drooping like lotuses
in the noonday sun?

And what is it now that scatters the tide
in the shadow of this proud watercourse?
The ridicule of the dead?
Susurrant sails still whisper
legends on the horizon: who are you,
occupant of the silent sigh of the conch?
The ground seems only a memory now, a torn breath.
and as we wait for the tide to flood the mudflats
the song that reaches our ears is just our own.
The cries of fishermen come drifting through the spray
music of what the world has lost.

JAYANTA MAHAPATRA

4. MEN AND WOMEN

SEVEN AGES OF MAN

All the world's a stage,
And all the men and women merely players:
They have their exits and their entrances;
And one man in his time plays many parts,
His acts being seven ages. At first the infant,
Mewling and puking in the nurse's arms.
And then the whining school-boy, with his satchel
And shining morning face, creeping like snail
Unwillingly to school. And then the lover,
Sighing like furnace, with a woeful ballad
Made to his mistress' eyebrow. Then a soldier,
Full of strange oaths, and bearded like the pard,
Jealous in honour, sudden and quick in quarrel,
Seeking the bubble reputation
Even in the cannon's mouth. And then the justice,
In fair round belly with good capon lin'd,
With eyes severe, and beard of formal cut,
Full of wise saws and modern instances;
And so he plays his part. The sixth age shifts
Into the lean and slipper'd pantaloon,
With spectacles on nose and pouch on side,
His youthful hose well sav'd a world too wide
For his shrunk shank; and his big manly voice,
Turning again toward childish treble, pipes
And whistles in his sound. Last scene of all,
That ends this strange eventful history,
Is second childishness and mere oblivion,
Sans teeth, sans eyes, sans taste, sans everything.
                    WILLIAM SHAKESPEARE (*As You Like It*)

THE VILLAGE BLACKSMITH

Under a spreading chestnut tree
  The village smithy stands;
The smith, a mighty man is he,
  With large and sinewy hands;
And the muscles of his brawny arms
  Are strong as iron bands.

His hair is crisp, and black, and long,
  His face is like the tan;
His brow is wet with honest sweat,
  He earns whate'er he can,
And looks the whole world in the face.
  For he owes not any man.

Week in, week out, from morn till night,
  You can hear his bellows blow;
You can hear him swing his heavy sledge,
  With measured beat and slow,
Like a sexton ringing the village bell,
  When the evening sun is low.

And children coming home from school
  Look in at the open door;
They love to see the flaming forge,
  And hear the bellows roar,
And catch the burning sparks that fly
  Like chaff from a threshing floor.

He goes on Sunday to the church,
  And sits among his boys;
He hears the parson pray and preach,
  He hears his daughter's voice
Singing in the village choir,
  And it makes his heart rejoice.

It sounds to him like her mother's voice,
  Singing in Paradise!

He needs must think of her once more,
    How in the grave she lies;
And with his hard, rough hand he wipes
    A tear out of his eyes.

Toiling—rejoicing,—sorrowing,
    Onward through life he goes;
Each morning sees some task begin,
    Each evening sees it close;
Something attempted, something done,
    Has earned a night's repose.

Thanks, thanks to thee, my worthy friend,
    For the lesson thou hast taught!
Thus at the flaming forge of life
    Our fortunes must be wrought;
Thus on its sounding anvil shaped
    Each burning deed and thought!
              HENRY WADSWORTH LONGFELLOW

THE VILLAGE SCHOOLMASTER

Beside yon straggling fence that skirts the way
With blossomed furze unprofitably gay,
There, in his noisy mansion, skilled to rule,
The village master taught his little school;
A man severe he was, and stern to view,
I knew him well, and every truant knew;
Well had the boding tremblers learned to trace
The day's disasters in his morning face;
Full well they laughed, with counterfeited glee,
At all his jokes, for many a joke had he;
Full well the busy whisper, circling round,
Conveyed the dismal tidings when he frowned;
Yet he was kind, or if severe in aught,
The love he bore to learning was in fault;
The village all declared how much he knew;
'Twas certain he could write, and cipher too;
Lands he could measure, terms and tides presage,

And even the story ran that he could gauge.
In arguing, too, the parson owned his skill,
For, even though vanquished, he could argue still;
While words of learned length and thundering sound
Amazed the gazing rustics ranged around;
And still they gazed, and still the wonder grew
That one small head could carry all he knew.

OLIVER GOLDSMITH

THE SOLITARY REAPER

Behold her, single in the field,
   Yon solitary Highland Lass!
Reaping and singing by herself;
   Stop here, or gently pass!
Alone she cuts and binds the grain,
And sings a melancholy strain;
O listen! for the vale profound
Is overflowing with the sound.

No nightingale did ever chaunt
   More welcome notes to weary bands
Of travellers in some shady haunt,
   Among Arabian sands:
A voice so thrilling ne'er was heard
In spring-time from the cuckoo-bird.
Breaking the silence of the seas
Among the farthest Hebrides.

Will no one tell me what she sings?—
   Perhaps the plaintive numbers flow
For old, unhappy, far-off things,
   And battles long ago:
Or is it some more humble lay
Familiar matter of to-day?
Some natural sorrow, loss, or pain,
That has been and may be again?

Whate'er the theme, the maiden sang
   As if her song could have no ending
I saw her singing at her work,
   And o'er the sickle bending;—
I listened, motionless and still;
And, as I mounted up the hill,
The music in my heart I bore
Long after it was heard no more.

            WILLIAM WORDSWORTH

LORD ULLIN'S DAUGHTER

A chieftain to the Highlands bound
Cries 'Boatman, do not tarry!
And I'll give thee a silver pound
To row us o'er the ferry!'

Now who be ye, would cross Lochgyle
This dark and stormy water?'
O I'm the chief of Ulva's isle,
And this, lord Ullin's daughter.

'And fast before her father's men
Three days we've fled together,
For should he find us in the glen;
My blood would stain the heather.

His horsemen hard behind us ride—
Should they our steps discover,
Then who will cheer my bonny bride
When they have slain her lover?'

Out spoke the hardy Highland wight,
'I'll go, my chief, I'm ready:
It is not for your silver bright,
But for your winsome lady:—

'And by my word! the bonny bird
In danger shall not tarry;
So though the waves are raging white
I'll row you o'er the ferry.'

By this the storm grew loud apace,
The water-wraith was shrieking;
And in the scowl of heaven each face
Grew dark as they were speaking.

But still as wilder blew the wind
And as the night grew drearer,
Adown the glen rode armed men,
Their trampling sounded nearer.

'O haste thee, haste!' the lady cries,
'Though tempests round us gather;
I'll meet the raging of the skies,
But not an angry father.'

The boat has left a stormy land,
A stormy sea before her,—
When, O! too strong for human hand
The tempest gather'd o'er her.

And still they row'd amidst the roar
Of waters fast prevailing:
Lord Ullin reach'd that fatal shore,—
His wrath was changed to wailing.

For, sore dismay'd, through storm and shade
His child he did discover:—
One lovely hand she stretch'd for aid.
And one was round her lover.

'Come back! come back!' he cried in grief
'Across this stormy water:
And I'll forgive your Highland chief,
My daughter!—O my daughter!'

'Twas vain: the loud waves lash'd the shore,
Return or aid preventing:

The waters wild went o'er his child,
And he was left lamenting.

SIR THOMAS CAMPBELL

THE SCHOLAR

My days among the Dead are past;
   Around me I behold.
Where'er these casual eyes are cast,
   The mighty minds of old:
My never-failing friends are they,
With whom I converse day by day.

With them I take delight in weal
   And seek relief in woe;
And while I understand and feel
   How much to them I owe,
My cheeks have often been bedew'd
With tears of thoughtful gratitude.

My thoughts are with the Dead; with them
   I live in long-past years.
Their virtues love, their faults condemn,
   Partake their hopes and fears,
And from their lessons seek and find
Instruction with an humble mind.

My hopes are with the Dead; anon
   My place with them will be.
And I with them shall travel on
   Through all Futurity;
Yet leaving here a name, I trust,
That will not perish in the dust.

ROBERT SOUTHEY

ABOU BEN ADHEM

Abou Ben Adhem (may his tribe increase')
Awoke one night from a deep dream of peace,

And saw, within the moonlight in his room
Making it rich, and like a lily in bloom,
An angel writing in a book of gold:—
Exceeding peace had made Ben Adhem bold,
And to the presence in the room he said,
    'What writest thou?'—The vision rais'd its head,
And with a look made of all sweet accord,
Answer'd, 'The names of those who love the Lord.'
'And is mine one?' said Abou. 'Nay, not so,'
Replied the angel. Abou spoke more low,
But cheerly still; and said, 'I pray thee, then,
Write me as one that loves his fellow men.'
    The angel wrote, and vanish'd. The next night
It came again with a great wakening light,
And show'd the names whom love of God had blest,
And lo! Ben Adhem's name led all the rest.

JAMES LEIGH HUNT

THE VAGABOND

Give to me the life I love,
    Let the lave go by me,
Give the jolly heaven above
    And the by-way nigh me.
Bed in the bush with stars to see,
    Bread I dip in the river—
There's the life for a man like me,
    There's the life for ever.

Let the blow fall soon or late,
    Let what will be o'er me;
Give the face of earth around
    And the road before me.
Wealth I seek not, hope nor love,
    Nor a friend to know me;
All I seek, the heaven above,
    And the road below me

Or let autumn fall on me
   Where afield I linger,
Silencing the bird on tree,
   Biting the blue finger.
White as meal the frosty field—
   Warm the fireside haven—
Not to autumn will I yield,
   Not to winter even!

Let the blow fall soon or late,
   Let what will be o'er me;
Give the face of earth around,
   And the road before me.
Wealth I ask not, hope nor love,
   Nor a friend to know me.
All I ask, the heaven above,
   And the road below me.

     Robert Louis Stevenson

SITA

Three happy children in a darkened room!
What do they gaze on with wide-open eyes?
A dense, dense forest, where no sunbeam pries',
And in its centre a cleared spot.—There bloom
Gigantic flowers on creepers that embrace
Tall trees; there, in a quiet lucid lake
The white swans glide; there, 'whirring from the brake.
The peacock springs; there, herds of wild deer race;
There, patches gleam with yellow waving grain;
There, blue smoke from strange altars rises light,
There, dwells in peace the poet-anchorite.
But who is this fair lady? Not in vain
She weeps.—for lo! at every tear she sheds
Tears from three pairs of young eyes fall amain,
And bowed in sorrow are the three young heads.
It is an old, old story, and the lay
Which has evoked sad Sita from the past

Is by a mother sung... 'Tis hushed at last
And melts the picture from their sight away,
Yet shall they dream of it until the day!
When shall those children by their mother's side
Gather, ah me! as erst at eventide?

Toru Dutt

5. LOVE

THE SUN RISING

Busy old fool, unruly Sun,
Why dost thou thus,
Through windows and through curtains call on us?
Must to thy motions lovers' seasons run?
Saucy pedantic wretch, go chide
Late school-boys, and sour 'prentices,
Go tell court-huntsmen that the King will ride,
Call country ants to harvest offices;
Love, all alike, no season knows, nor clime.
Nor hours, days, months, which are the rags of time

Thy beams, so reverend and strong
Why shouldst thou think?
I could eclipse and cloud them with a wink,
But that I would not lose her sight so long:
If her eyes have not blinded thine.
Look, and tomorrow late tell me,
Whether both the Indias of spice and mine
Be where thou left'st them, or lie here with me.
Ask for those kings whom thou saw'st yesterday,
And thou shalt hear, 'All here in one bed lay.'

She's all States, and all Princes I;
Nothing else is.
Princes do but play us; compared to this,
All honour's mimic; all wealth alchemy.
Thou, Sun, art half as happy as we,
In that the world's contracted thus;
Thine age asks ease, and since thy duties be
To warm the world, that's done in warming us.
Shine here to us, and thou art everywhere;
This bed thy centre is, these walls thy sphere.

JOHN DONNE

THE NIGHT PIECE: TO JULIA

Her eyes the glow-worm lend thee,
The shooting stars attend thee;
    And the elves also,
     Whose little eyes glow
Like the sparks of fire, befriend thee.

No Will-o'-th'-Wisp mislight thee,
Nor snake or slow-worm bite thee;
    But oh, on thy way
    Not making a stay,
Since ghost there's none to affright thee

Let not the dark thee cumber:
What though the moon does slumber?
    The stars of the night
    Will lend thee their light,
Like tapers clear without number.

ROBERT HERRICK

JOHN ANDERSON MY JO

John Anderson my jo, John,
  When we were first acquent;
Your locks were like the raven.
  Your bony brow was brent;
But now your brow is beld, John.
  Your locks are like the snaw;
But blessings on your frosty pow,
  John Anderson my Jo.

John Anderson my jo, John
  We clamb the hill the gither;
And mony a canty day, John.
  We've had wi' ane anither:
Now we maun totter down, John,
  And hand in hand we'll go;

And sleep the gither at the foot,
    John Anderson my Jo.

ROBERT BURNS

SHE WALKS IN BEAUTY

She walks in beauty, like the night
    Of cloudless climes and starry skies;
And all that's best of dark and bright
    Meet in her aspect and her eyes:
Thus mellow'd to that tender light
    Which heaven to gaudy day denies.

One shade the more, one ray the less,
    Had half impair'd the nameless grace
Which waves in every raven tress,
    Or softly lightens o'er her face;
Where thoughts serenely sweet express
    How pure, how dear their dwelling-place.

And on that cheek, and o'er that brow,
    So soft, so calm, yet eloquent,
The smiles that win, the tints that glow
    But tell of days in goodness spent,
A mind at peace with all below,
    A heart whose love is innocent.

GEORGE GORDON NOEL, LORD BYRON

BELIEVE ME, IF ALL THOSE ENDEARING YOUNG CHARMS

Believe me, if all those endearing young charms
        Which I gaze on so fondly to-day
Were to change by to-morrow, and fleet in my arms,
        Like fairy-gifts fading away,
Thou wouldst still be adored, as this moment thou art,
        Let thy loveliness fade as it will;

And around the dear ruin each wish of my heart
    Would entwine itself verdantly still.

It is not while beauty and youth are thine own,
    And thy cheeks unprofaned by a tear;
That the fervour and faith of a Soul can be known
    To which time will but make thee more dear;
No, the heart that has truly loved never forgets,
    But as truly loves on to the close
As the sunflower turns on his god when he sets
    The same look which she turned when he rose..

THOMAS MOORE

HIAWATHA'S WOOING

(From the "Song of Hiawatha")

  "As unto the bow the cord is,
So unto the man is woman;
Though she bends him, she obeys him,
Though she draws him, yet she follows;
Useless each without the other!"

    Thus the youthful Hiawatha
Said within himself and pondered,
Much perplexed by various feelings,
Listless, longing, hoping, fearing,
Dreaming still of Minnehaha,
Of the lovely Laughing Water.
In the land of the Dacotahs.

    "Wed a maiden of your people,"
Warning said the old Nokomis;
"Go not eastward, go not westward,
For a stranger, whom we know not!
Like a fire upon the hearth-stone
Is a neighbor's homely daughter,
Like the starlight or the moonlight
Is the handsomest of strangers!"

Thus dissuading spake Nokomis,
And my Hiawatha answered
Only this: "Dear old Nokomis,
Very pleasant is the firelight,
But I like the starlight better,
Better do I like the moonlight!"

Gravely then said old Nokomis:
"Bring not here an idle maiden,
Bring not here a useless woman,
Hands unskilful, feet unwilling;
Bring a wife with nimble fingers,
Heart and hand that move together,
Feet that run on willing errands!"

Smiling answered Haiwatha:
"In the land of the Dacotahs
Lives the Arrow-maker s daughter,
Minnehaha, Laughing Water,
Handsomest of all the women.
I will bring her to your wigwam,
She shall run upon your errands,
Be your starlight, moonlight, firelight,
Be your sunlight of my people!"

Still dissuading said Nokomis:
"Bring not to my lodge a stranger
From the land of the Dacotahs!
Very fierce are the Dacotahs,
Often is there war between us,
There are feuds, yet unforgotten,
Wounds that ache and still may open!"

Laughing answered Hiawatha:
"For that reason-, if no other,
Would I wed the fair Dacotah,
That our tribes might be united,
That old feuds might be forgotten,
And old wounds be healed forever!'

Thus departed Hiawatha

To the land of the Dacotahs,
To the land of handsome women;
Striding over moor and meadow,
Through interminable forests,
Through uninterrupted silence.

With his moccasins of magic,
At each stride a mile he measured;
Yet the way seemed long before him,
And his heart outran his footsteps;
And he journeyed without resting,
Till he heard the cataract's laughter,
Heard the Falls of Minnehaha
Calling to him through the silence.
"Pleasant is the sound!" he murmured,
"Pleasant is the voice that calls me!"

On the outskirts of the forests,
'Twixt the shadow and the sunshine,
Herds of fallow deer were feeding.
But they saw not Hiawatha;
To his bow he whispered. "Fail not!"
To his arrow whispered, "Swerve not!"
Sent it singing on its errand.
To the red heart of the roebuck;
Threw the deer across his shoulder.
And sped forward without pausing.

At the doorway of his wigwam
Sat the ancient Arrow-maker,
In the land of the Dacotahs,
Making arrow-heads of jasper.
Arrow-heads of chalcedony.
At his side, in all her beauty.
Sat the lovely Minnehaha,
Sat his daughter. Laughing Water,
Plaiting mats of flags and rushes;
Of the past the old man's thoughts were,
And the maiden's of the future.

He was thinking, as he sat there,

Of the days when with such arrows
He had struck the deer and bison
On the Muskoday, the meadow;
Shot the wild goose, flying southward.
On the wing, the clamorous Wawa;
Thinking of the great war-parties,
How they came to buy his arrows,
Could not fight without his arrows,
Ah, no more such noble warriors
Could be found on earth as they were!
Now the men were all like women,
Only used their tongues for weapons!

　She was thinking of a hunter,
From another tribe and country,
Young and tall and very handsome.
Who one morning, in the Spring-time,
Came to buy her father's arrows,
Sat and rested in the wigwam,
Lingered long about the doorway,
Looking back as he departed.
She had heard her father praise him,
Praise his courage and his wisdom;
Would he come again for arrows
To the Falls of Minnehaha?
On the mat her hands lay idle,
And her eyes were very dreamy.

　Through their thoughts they heard a footstep,
Heard a rustling in the branches.
And with glowing cheek and forehead,
With the deer upon his shoulders,
Suddenly from out the woodlands
Hiawatha stood before them.
Straight the ancient Arrow-maker
Looked up gravely from his labor,
Laid aside the unfinished arrow.
Bade him enter at the doorway,
Saying, as he rose to meet him,

"Hiawatha, you are welcome!"

At the feet of Laughing Water
Hiawatha laid his burden,
Threw the red deer from his shoulders;
And the maiden looked up at him,
Looked up from her mat of rushes.
Said with gentle look and accent,
"You are welcome, Haiwatha!"

Very spacious was the wigwam,
Made of deer-skins dressed and whitened,
With the Gods of the Dacotahs
Drawn and painted on its curtains,
And so tall the doorway, hardly
Hiawatha stooped to enter,
Hardly touched his eagle-feathers
As he entered at the doorway.

Then uprose the Laughing Water,
From the ground fair Minnehaha,
Laid aside her mat unfinished,
Brought forth food and set before them,
Water brought them from the brooklet,
Gave them food in earthen vessels,
Gave them drink in bowls of bass-wood,
Listened while the guest was speaking,
Listened while her father answered,
But not once her lips she opened,
Not a single word she uttered.

Yes, as in dream she listened
To the words of Hiawatha,
As he talked of old Nokomis,
Who had nursed him in his childhood,
As he told of his companions.
Chibiabos, the musician,
And the very strong man, Kwasind,
And of happiness and plenty
In the land of the Ojibways,

In the pleasant land and peaceful.

"After many years of warfare.
Many years of strife and bloodshed,
There is peace between the Ojibways
And the tribe of the Dacotahs."
Thus continued Hiawatha.
And then added, speaking slowly,
"That this peace may last forever,
And our hands be clasped more closely,
And our hearts be more united,
Give me as my wife this maiden,
Minnehaha, Laughing Water,
Loveliest of Dacotah women!"

And the ancient Arrow-maker
Paused a moment ere he answered,
Smoked a little while in silence,
Looked at Hiawatha proudly;
Fondly looked at Laughing Water,
And made answer very gravely:
"Yes, if Minnehaha wishes;
Let your heart speak, Minnehaha!"

And the lovely Laughing Water
Seemed more lovely as she stood there,
Neither willing nor reluctant,
As she went to Hiawatha,
Softly took the seat beside him,
While she said, and blushed to say it,
"I will follow you, my husband!"

This was Hiawatha's wooing!
Thus it was he won the daughter
Of the ancient Arrow-maker,
In the land of the Dacotahs!

From the wigwam he departed,
Leading with him Laughing Water;
Hand in hand they went together,
Through the woodland and the meadow,

Left the old man standing lonely
At the doorway of his wigwam,
Heard the Falls of Minnehaha
Calling to them from the distance,
Crying to them from afar off,
"Fare thee well, O Minnehaha!"

    And the ancient Arrow-maker
Turned again unto his labor,
Sat down by his sunny doorway
Murmuring to himself, and saying:
"Thus it is our daughters leave us,
Those we love, and those who love us!
Just when they have learned to help us,
When we are old and lean upon them,
Comes a youth with flaunting feathers,
With his flute of reeds, a stranger
Wanders piping through the village,
Beckons to the fairest maiden,
And she follows where he leads her.
Leaving all things for the stranger!"

    Pleasant was the journey homeward,
Through interminable forests,
Over meadow, over mountain,
Over river, hill, and hollow.
Short it seemed to Hiawatha,
Though they journeyed very slowly,
Though his pace he checked and slackened
To the steps of Laughing Water.

    Over wide and rushing rivers
In his arms he bore the maiden;
Light he thought her as a feather,
As the plume upon his head-gear;
Cleared the tangled pathway for her,
Bent aside the swaying branches,
Made at night a lodge of branches,
And a bed with boughs of hemlock,
And a fire before the doorway

With the dry cones of the pine-tree.

All the traveling winds went with them,
O'er the meadows, through the forest;
All the stars of night looked at them,
Watched with sleepless eyes their slumber;
From his ambush in the oak-tree
Peeped the squirrel, Adjidaumo,
Watched with eager eyes the loyers;
And the rabbit, the Wabasso,
Scampered from the path before them.
Peering, peeping from his burrow,
Sat erect upon his haunches,
Watched with curious eyes the lovers.

Pleasant was the journey homeward!
All the birds sang loud and sweetly
Songs of happiness and heart's-ease;
Sang the bluebird, the Owaissa,
"Happy are you, Hiawatha.
Having now a wife to love you!"
Sang the robin, the Opechee,
"Happy are you, Laughing Water,
Having such a noble husband!"

From the sky the sun benignant
Looked upon them through the branches,
Saying to them, "O my children,
Love is sunshine, hate is shadow,
Life is checkered shade and sunshine,
Rule by love, O Hiawatha!"

From the sky the moon looked at them,
Filled the lodge with mystic splendors,
Whispered to them, "O my children,
Day is restless, night is quiet;
Man imperious, woman feeble;
Half is mine, although I follow;
Rule by patience, Laughing Water!"

Thus it was they journeyed homeward;

Thus it was that Hiawatha
To the lodge of old Nokomis
Brought the moonlight, starlight, firelight,
Brought the sunshine of his people,
Minnehaha, Laughing Water,
Handsomest of all the women
In the land of the Dacotahs,
In the land of handsome women.

HENRY WADSWORTH LONGFELLOW

LINES TO AN INDIAN AIR

I arise from dreams of thee
    In the first sweet sleep of night,
When the winds are breathing low
    And the stars are shining bright:
I arise from dreams of thee,
    And a spirit in my feet
Has led me—who knows how?
    To thy chamber-window. Sweet!

The wandering airs they faint
    On the dark, the silent stream—
The champak odours fail
    Like sweet thoughts in a dream;
The nightingale's complaint
    It dies upon her heart.
As I must die on thine,
    O beloved as thou art!

O lift me from the grass!
    I die! I faint! I fail!
Let thy love in kisses rain
    On my lips and eyelids pale.
My cheek is cold and white, alas!
    My heart beats loud and fast;
O! press it close to thine again
    Where it will break at last.

PERCY BYSSHE SHELLEY

SHE IS NOT FAIR TO OUTWARD VIEW

She is not fair to outward view
   As many maidens be;
Her loveliness I never knew
   Until she smiled on me.
O then I saw her eye was bright,
A well of love, a spring of light.

But now her looks are coy and cold,
   To mine they ne'er reply
And yet I cease not to behold
   The love-light in her eye:
Her very frowns are fairer far
Than smiles of other maidens are.

HARTLEY COLERIDGE

MY GRANDMOTHER'S HOUSE

There is a house now far away where once
I received love......That woman died,
The house withdrew into silence, snakes moved
Among books I was then too young
To read, and, my blood turned cold like the moon.
How often I think of going
There, to peer through blind eyes of windows or
Just listen to the frozen air,
Or in wild despair, pick an armful of
Darkness to bring it here to lie
Behind my bedroom door like a brooding
Dog......you cannot believe, darling,
Can you, that I lived in such a house and
Was proud, and loved......I who have lost
My way and beg now at strangers' doors to
Receive love, at least in small change?

KAMALA DAS

6. BALLADS AND NARRATIVES

LOCHINVAR

O, young Lochinvar is come out of the west,
Through all the wide Border his steed was the best;
And save his good broadsword he weapons had none,
He rode all unarm'd, and he rode all alone.
So faithful in love, and so dauntless in war,
There never was knight like the young Lochinvar.

He staid not for brake, and he stopp'd not for stone,
He swam the Eske river where ford there was none;
But ere he alighted at Netherby gate,
The bride had consented, the gallant came late:
For a laggard in love, and a dastard in war,
Was to wed the fair Ellen of brave Lochinvar.

So boldly he enter'd the Netherby Hall,
Among bride's-men, and kinsmen, and brothers, and all:
Then spoke the bride's father, his hand on his sword,
(For the poor craven bridegroom said never a word)
'O come ye in peace here, or come ye in war,
Or to dance at our bridal, young Lord Lochinvar?'

'I long woo'd your daughter, my suit you denied;—
Love swells like the Solway, but ebbs like its tide—
And now am I come, with this lost love of mine,
To lead but one measure, drink one cup of wine.
There are maidens in Scotland more lovely by far,
That would gladly be bride to the young Lochinvar.'

The bride kiss'd the goblet: the knight took it up,
He quaff'd off the wine, and he threw down the cup.
She look'd down to blush, and she look'd up to sigh,
With a smile on her lips, and a tear in her eye.

He took her soft hand, ere her mother could bar,—
'Now tread we a measure!' said young Lochinvar.

So stately his form, and so lovely her face,
That never a hall such a galliard did grace;
While her mother did fret, and her father did fume,
And the bridegroom stood dangling his bonnet and plume;
And the bride-maidens whisper'd, "Twere better by far,
To have match'd our fair cousin with your Lochinvar.'

One touch to her hand, and one word in her ear,
When they reach'd the hall-door, and the charger stood near;
So light to the croup the fair lady he swung,
So light to the saddle before her he sprung!
'She is won! we are gone, over bank, bush, and scaur;
They'll have fleet steeds that follow,' quoth young Lochinvar.

There was mounting 'mong Graemes of the Netherby clan;
Forsters, Fenwicks, and Musgraves, they rode and they ran:
There was racing and chasing on Cannobie Lee.
But the lost bride of Netherby ne'er did they see.
So daring in love, and so dauntless in war,
Have ye e'er heard of gallant like young Lochinvar?

SIR WALTER SCOTT

A MINOR SACRIFICE

(remembering the dead in My Lai 4)

i

I'd just heard that day
of the mischievous king in the epic
who kills a snake in the forest
and thinks it would be such fun
to garland a sage's neck
with the cold dead thing,
and so he does,
and promptly earns a curse,
an early death by snakebite.
His son vows vengeance

and performs a sacrifice,
a magic rite
that draws every snake from everywhere,
till snakes of every stripe
begin to fall
through the blazing air
into his altar fires.

Then that day, Uncle, of all people,
a man who shudders at silk,
for he loves the worm,
who would never hurt a fly
but catch it most gently
to look at it eye to eye
and let it go,

suddenly strikes our first summer scorpion
on the wall next to Gopu's bed
with the ivory dragonhead
of his walking stick
and shows us the ripe
yellow poison-bead
behind the sting.

Grandmother then, tut-tutting
like a lizard,
tells us how a pregnant scorpion
will look for a warm secret place,
say, a little girl's underwear
or a little boy's jockstrap,
and then will burst her back
to let loose in her death
a host of baby scorpions.

'They're quite red at birth,
the little ones'. Uncle says.
'They glow like hand-carved rubies
from Peking, redder than garnet,
especially when you hold them up

to the light.
And when they grow big,
they take on the colour of gray
China jade. Beautiful, beautiful',
he says, shaking his marmoset head

ii

That afternoon, Shivanna asks me
under the sighing neem tree,
'Wouldn't you like to rid the world
of scorpions, if you could?'
'Yes, but how?'

           'Witchcraft', says he
shining darker than an ebony turtle.
'We can make them come at our bidding
when the sun is in Scorpio,
like guests to a wedding,
into the bole of this very tree.
And they will burn in a bonfire
you and I will light.'

           'What, all of them?
'Yes, and every kind. Black, red,
white, yellow, young, old,
the three-legged and the blind.'

'Can we do it now?'

           'Not so fast, kiddo.
What can you get without a sacrifice?
First, we've to feed
the twelve-handed god of scorpions
something he loves as other gods
love goats and rice.
For that, you need
one hundred live grasshoppers
caught on a newmoon Tuesday.
But remember: no wings on those things.
Catch them next Tuesday,
and I'll show you twigs on this tree

that will drip with scorpion legs.'
'Will you come with me?'
                                    'No', he says.
'I'm busy. Take Gopu with you.
You'll need three jars.'

                        iii

So we steal three pickle jars at dawn
on that breezy newmoon Tuesday.
Leaping and hopping all over the lawn.

we become expert by noon
at the common art
of catching grasshoppers on the wing,

learning by the way
to tell apart
twigs and twiglike insects

that turn slowly round the twigs,
shamming dead
at the touch of a mere look,

as if it could burn.

We unlearn
what we couldn't have in years,
some small old fears

of other living things,
though we're still squeamish
when we pull of their wings

and shiver a bit
as we put away
those wriggles in our bottles.

And we learn,
as from no book,
the difficult art of counting

little writhing objects
through glass walls
with flaws and bubbles.

They had tiny compasses for thighs,
and moviestar goggles
for eyes.

iv

By evening we have ninety-nine.
The hardest is the last,
maybe because they too are learning.

But Gopu, who knows by heart the score
of every Test Match,
stalks and pounces in the half dark.

Breathless, he almost crushes his catch.
So we make our century,
sneak by the backdoor

to the bath house
to scrub and scour with coconut fibre
till the skins of our palms come off.

That night we don't eat or sleep too well.
We draw sticks and it falls to Gopu's lot
to keep the jars of grasshopper cripples safe

under his bed
and even that savage innocent
dreams all night

of every punishment
in the narrow woodcut columns
of the yellowing almanacs of Hindu hells.

V

When we go to see Shivanna
on Wednesday morning,
the jars behind our backs,
most of the grasshoppers
rather still or very slow.

Shivanna's mother tells us
he is in the hospital
taken sick with some strange
twitching disease.

We never see him alive again.
Uncle says, later,
                          'Did you know, that Shivanna,
he clawed and kicked the air
all that day, that newmoon Tuesday,
like some bug
on its back?'

A.K. RAMANUJAN

THE INCHCAPE ROCK

No stir in the air, no stir in the sea,
The ship was as still as she could be,
Her sails from heaven received no motion,
Her keel was steady in the ocean.

Without either sign or sound of their shock,
The waves flowed over the Inchcape Rock;
So little they rose, so little they fell.
They did not move the Inchcape Bell.

The good old Abbot of Aberbrothok,
Had placed that bell on the Inchcape Rock;
On a buoy in the storm it floated and swung,
And over the waves its warning rung.

When the Rock was hid by the surges' swell,
The mariners heard the warning bell;

And then they knew the perilous Rock,
And blest the Abbot of Aberbrothok,

The sun in heaven was shining gay,
All things were joyful on that day;
The sea-birds screamed as they wheeled round,
And there was joyance in their sound.

The buoy of the Inchcape Bell was seen
A darker speck on the ocean green;
Sir Ralph the Rover walked his deck,
And he fixed his eyes on the darker speck.

He felt the cheering power of spring,
It made him whistle, it made him sing;
His heart was mirthful to excess,
But the Rover's mirth was wickedness.

His eye was on the Inchcape float;
Quoth he. 'My men, put out the boat,
And row me to the Inchcape Rock,
And I'll plague the priest of Aberbrothok.'

The boat is lowered, the boatmen row,
And to the Inchcape Rock they go;
Sir Ralph bent over from the boat.
And he cut the bell from the Inchcape float.

Down sunk the bell, with a gurgling sound,
The bubbles rose and burst around;
Quoth Sir Ralph, 'The next who comes to the Rock
Won't bless the Abbot of Aberbrothok.'

Sir Ralph the Rover sailed away,
He scoured the seas for many a day;
And now grown rich with plundered store,
He steers his course for Scotland's shore

So thick a haze o'erspreads the sky,
They cannot see the sun on high;
The wind hath blown a gale all day,
At evening it hath died away

On deck the Rover takes his stand,
So dark it is they see no land,
Quoth Sir Ralph, 'It will be lighter soon,
For there is the dawn of the rising moon.'

'Canst hear,' said one, 'the breakers roar?
For methinks we should be near the shore.'
'Now where we are I cannot tell,
But I wish I could hear the Inchcape Bell.'

They hear no sound, the swell is strong;
Though the wind hath fallen, they drift along,
Till the vessel strikes with a shivering shock;—
'O Christ! It is the Inchcape Rock.'

Sir Ralph the Rover tore his hair,
He cursed himself in his despair;
The waves rushed in on every side,
The ship is sinking beneath the tide.

But even in his dying fear
One dreadful sound could the Rover hear,
A sound as if with the Inchcape Bell.
The Devil below was ringing his knell

ROBERT SOUTHEY

THE SLAVE'S DREAM

Beside the ungathered rice he lay,
    His sickle in his hand;
His breast was bare, his matted hair
    Was buried in the sand.
Again, in the mist and shadow of sleep,
    He saw his Native Land.

Wide through the landscape of his dreams
    The lordly Niger flowed;
Beneath the palm-trees on the plain
    Once more a king he strode;
And heard the tinkling caravans
    Descend the mountain-road.

He saw once more his dark-eyed queen
　　Among her children stand;
They clasped his neck, they kissed his cheeks,
　　They held him by the hand!—
A tear burst from the sleeper's lids
　　And fell into the sand.

And then at furious speed he rode
　　Along the Niger's bank;
His bridle-reins were golden chains,
　　And, with a martial clank.
At each leap he could feel his scabbard of steel
　　Smiting his stallion's flank.

Before him, like a blood-red flag.
　　The bright flamingoes flew;
From morn till night he followed their flight,
　　O'er plains where the tamarind grew,
Till he saw the roofs of Caffre huts,
　　And the ocean rose to view.

At night he heard the lion roar,
　　And the hyena scream,
And the river-horse, as he crushed the reeds
　　Beside some hidden stream;
And it passed, like a glorious roll of drums,
　　Through the triumph of his dream.

The forests, with their myriad tongues,
　　Shouted of Liberty;
And the blast of the Desert cried aloud,
　　With a voice so wild and free,
That he started in his sleep and smiled
　　At their tempestuous glee.

He did not feel the driver's whip,
　　Nor the burning heat of day;
For Death had illumined the Land of Sleep,
　　And his lifeless body lay
A worn-out fetter, that the soul

Had broken and thrown away!
HENRY WADSWORTH LONGFELLOW

THE PIED PIPER OF HAMELIN

I

Hamelin Town's in Brunswick,
   By famous Hanover city;
The River Weser, deep and wide,
Washes its wall on the southern side;
A pleasanter spot you never spied;
   But when begins my ditty,
Almost five hundred years ago,
To see the townsfolk suffer so
   From vermin, was a pity.

II

   Rats!
They fought the dogs and killed the cats,
   And bit the babies in the cradles,
And ate the cheeses out of the vats,
   And licked the soup from the cooks' own ladles,
Split open the kegs of salted sprats,
Made nests inside men's Sunday hats,
And even spoiled the women's chats
    By drowning their speaking
    With shrieking and squeaking
In fifty different sharps and flats.

III

At last the people in a body
   To the Town Hall came flocking:
''Tis clear,' cried they, 'our Mayor's a noddy;
   And as for our Corporation—shocking
To think we buy gowns lined with ermine
For dolts that can't or won't determine
What's best to rid us of our vermin!

You hope, because you're old and obese,
To find in the furry civic robe ease?
Rouse up, Sirs! Give your brains a racking
To find the remedy we're lacking,
Or, sure as fate, we'll send you packing!'
At this the Mayor and Corporation
Quaked with a mighty consternation.

IV

An hour they sat in council,
   At length the Mayor broke silence:
'For a guilder I'd my ermine gown sell;
   I wish I were a mile hence!
It's easy to bid one rack one's brain—
I'm sure my poor head aches again,
I've scratched it so, and all in vain.
O for a trap, a trap, a trap!'
Just as he said this, what should hap
At the chamber door, but a gentle tap?
'Bless us!' cried the Mayor, 'what's that?'
(With the Corporation as he sat,
Looking little though wondrous fat;
Nor brighter was his eye, nor moister
Than a too-long-opened oyster,
Save when at noon his paunch grew mutinous
For a plate of turtle green and glutinous)
'Only a scraping of shoes on the mat?
Anything like the sound of a rat
Makes my heart go pit-a-pat!'

V

'Come in!'—the Mayor cried, looking bigger:
And in did come the strangest figure!
His queer long coat from heel to head
Was half of yellow and half of red,
And he himself was tall and thin,
With sharp blue eyes, each like a pin,
And light loose hair, yet swarthy skin,

No tuft on cheek nor beard on chin,
But lips where smiles went out and in;
There was no guessing his kith and kin:
And nobody could enough admire
The tall man and his quaint attire.
Quoth one: 'It's as my great-grandsire,
Starting up at the Trump of Doom's tone,
Had walked this way from his painted tomb-stone!'

VI

He advanced to the council-table:
And, 'Please your honours,' said he, 'I'm able,
By means of a secret charm, to draw
    All creatures living beneath the sun,
    That creep or swim or fly or run,
After me so as you never saw!
And I chiefly use my charm
On creatures that do people harm,
The mole and toad and newt and viper;
And people call me the Pied Piper.'
(And here they noticed round his neck
    A scarf of red and yellow stripe
To match with his coat of the self-same cheque;
And at the scarf's end hung a pipe;
And his fingers, they noticed, were ever straying
As if impatient to be playing
Upon his pipe, as low it dangled
Over his vesture so old-fangled.)
'Yet,' said he, 'poor piper as I am,
In Tartary I freed the Cham,
    Last June, from his huge swarms of gnats;
I eased in Asia the Nizam
    Of a monstrous brood of vampyre-bats:
And as for what your brain bewilders,
    If I can rid your town of rats
Will you give me a thousand guilders?'
'One? fifty thousand!'—was the exclamation
Of the astonished Mayor and Corporation,

VII

Into the street the Piper stept.
   Smiling first a little smile,
As if he knew what magic slept
   In his quiet pipe the while;
Then, like a musical adept,
To blow the pipe his lips he wrinkled,
And green and blue his sharp eyes twinkled,
Like a candle-flame where salt is sprinkled;
And ere three shrill notes the pipe uttered,
You heard as if an army muttered;
And the muttering grew to a grumbling;
And the grumbling grew to a mighty rumbling;
And out of the houses the rats came tumbling.
Great rats, small rats, lean rats, brawny rats,
Brown rats, black rats, grey rats, tawny rats,
Grave old plodders, gay young friskers,
   Fathers, mothers, uncles, cousins,
Cocking tails and pricking whiskers,
   Families by tens and dozens,
Brothers, sisters, husbands, wives—
Followed the Piper for their lives.
From street to street he piped advancing,
And step for step they followed dancing,
Until they came to the River Weser,
   Wherein all plunged and perished!
—Save one who, stout as Julius Caesar,
Swam across and lived to carry
   (As he, the manuscript he cherished)
To Rat-land home his commentary:
Which was, 'As the first shrill notes of the pipe,
I heard a sound as of scraping tripe,
And putting apples, wondrous ripe,
Into a cider-press's gripe:
And a moving away of pickle-tub-boards,
And a leaving ajar of conserve-cupboards,
And a drawing the corks of train-oil-flasks,
And a breaking the hoops of butter-casks:
And it seemed as if a voice

(Sweeter far than by harp or by psaltery
  Is breathed) called out, "Oh, rats, rejoice!
The world is grown to one vast drysaltery!
So munch on. crunch on, take your nuncheon,
Breakfast, supper, dinner, luncheon!"
And just as a bulky sugar-puncheon,
All ready staved, like a great sun shone
Glorious scarce an inch before me,
Just as methought it said, "Come, bore me!"
—I found the Weser rolling o'er me.'

VIII

You should have heard the Hamelin people
Ringing the bells till they rocked the steeple
'Go,' cried the Mayor, 'and get long poles,
Poke out the nests, and block up the holes!
Consult with carpenters and builders,
And leave in our town not even a trace
of the rats!'—when, suddenly, up the face
of the Piper perked in the market-place,
With a, 'First; if you please, my thousand guilders!'

IX

A thousand guilders! The Mayor looked blue;
So did the Corporation too.
For council dinners made rare havoc
With Claret, Moselle, Vin-de-Grave, Hock;
And half the money would replenish
Their cellar's biggest butt with Rhenish.
To pay this sum to a wandering fellow
With a gipsy coat of red and yellow!
'Beside,' quoth the Mayor, with a knowing wink,
'Our business was done at the river's brink;
We saw with our eyes the vermin sink,
And what's dead can't come to life, I think.
So, friend, we're not the folks to shrink
From the duty of giving you something for drink.
And a matter of money to put in your poke;

But as for the guilders, what we spoke
Of them, as you very well know, was in joke.
Beside, our losses have made us thrifty.
A thousand guilders! Come, take fifty!'

X

The Piper's face fell and he cried
'No trifling! I can't wait, beside!
I've promised to visit by dinner-time
Bagdat, and accept the prime
Of the Head-Cook's pottage, all he's rich in,
For having left, in Caliph's kitchen,
Of a nest of scorpions no survivor:
With him I proved no bargain-driver,
With you, don't think I'll bate a stiver!
And folks who put me in a passion
May find me pipe after another fashion.'

XI

'How?' cried the Mayor, 'd'ye think I brook
Being worse treated than a Cook?
Insulted by a lazy ribald
With idle pipe and vesture piebald?
You threaten us, fellow? Do your worst,
Blow your pipe there till you burst!'

XII

Once more he stept into the street
    And to his lips again
    Laid his long pipe of smooth straight cane;
And ere he blew three notes (such sweet
Soft notes as yet musician's cunning
    Never gave the enraptured air)
There was a rustling that seemed like a bustling,
Of merry crowds justling at pitching and hustling,
Small feet were pattering, wooden shoes clattering,
Little hands clapping and little tongues chattering,

And, like fowls in the farmyard when barley is scattering
Out came the children running.
All the little boys and girls,
With rosy cheeks and flaxen curls,
And sparkling eyes and teeth like pearls,
Tripping and skipping, ran merrily after
The wonderful music with shouting and laughter.

XIII

The Mayor was dumb, and the Council stood
As if they were changed into blocks of wood,
Unable to move a step, or cry
To the children merrily skipping by,
—Could only follow with the eye
That joyous crowd at the Piper's back.
But now the Mayor was on the rack,
And the wretched Council's bosoms beat,
As the Piper turned from the High Street
To where the Weser rolled its waters
Right in the way of their sons and daughters!
However, he turned from South to West,
And to Koppelberg hill his steps addressed,
And after him the children pressed;
Great was the joy in every breast.
'He never can cross that mighty top!
He's forced to let the piping drop,
And we shall see our children stop!'
When. lo. as they reached the mountain-side,
A wondrous portal opened wide.
As if a cavern was suddenly hollowed;
And the Piper advanced and the children followed,
And when all were in to the very last,
The door in the mountain-side shut fast.
Did I say all? No! One was lame,
    And could not dance the whole of the way;
And in after years, if you would blame
    His sadness, he was used to say,—
'It's dull in our town since my playmates left!
I can't forget that I'm bereft

Of all the pleasant sights they see,
Which the Piper also promised me.
For he led us, he said, to a joyous land,
Joining the town and just at hand,
Where waters gushed and fruit-trees grew
And flowers put forth a fairer hue,
And everything was strange and new;
The sparrows were brighter than peacocks here,
And their dogs outran our fallow deer,
And honey-bees had lost their stings,
And horses were born with eagles' wings:
And just as I became assured
My lame foot would be speedily cured,
The music stopped and I stood still,
And found myself outside the hill,
Left alone against my will,
To go now limping as before,
And never hear of that country more!'

XIV

Also, alas for Hamelin!
    There came into many a burgher's pate
    A text which says that heaven's gate
    Opens to the rich at as easy rate
As the needle's eye takes a camel in!
The Mayor sent East, West, North and South,
To offer the Piper, by word of mouth,
    Wherever it was men's lot to find him,
Silver and gold to his heart's content,
If he'd only return the way he went,
    And bring the children behind him.
But when they saw 'twas a lost endeavour,
And Piper and dancers were gone for ever.
They made a decree that lawyers never
    Should think their records dated duly
If, after the day of the month and the year,
These words did not as well appear,
'And so long after what happened here

On the Twenty-second of July,
Thirteen hundred and seventy-six:'
And the better in memory to fix
The place of the children's last retreat,
They called it 'The Pied Piper's Street —
Where any one playing on pipe or tabor
Was sure for the future to lose his labour.
Nor suffered they hostelry or tavern
To shock with mirth a street so solemn;
But opposite the place of the cavern
They wrote the story on a column,
And on the great church-window painted
The same, to make the world acquainted
How their children were stolen away,
And there it stands to this very day.
And I must not omit to say
That in Transylvania there's a tribe
Of alien people who ascribe
The outlandish ways and dress
On which their neighbours lay such stress,
To their fathers and mothers having risen
Out of some subterraneous prison
Into which they were trepanned
Long time ago in a mighty band
Out of Hamelin town in Brunswick land,
But how or why, they don't understand.

ROBERT BROWNING

THE BALLAD OF EAST AND WEST

Oh, East is East, and West is West, and never the twain shall meet,
Till Earth and Sky stand presently at God's great Judgment Seat;.
But there is neither East nor West, Border, nor Breed, nor Birth,
When two strong men stand face- to face, though they come from the ends of
*   the earth!*

Kamal is out with twenty men to raise the Borderside,
And he has lifted the Colonel's mare that is the Colonel's pride:

He has lifted her out of the stable-door between the dawn and the day,

And turned the calkins upon her feet, and ridden her far away.

Then up and spoke the Colonel's son that led a troop of the Guides:

'Is there never a man of all my men can say where Kamal hides?'

Then up and spoke Mahommed Khan, the son of the Ressaldar,

'If ye know the track of the morning-mist, ye know where his pickets are.

At dusk he harries the Abazai—at dawn he is into Bonair,

But he must go by Fort Bukloh to his own place to fare

So if ye gallop to Fort Bukloh as fast as a bird can fly,

By the favour of God ye may cut him off ere he win to the Tongue of Jagai.

But if he be past the Tongue of Jagai, right swiftly turn ye then,

For the length and the breadth of that grisly plain is sown with Kamal's men.

There is rock to the left, and rock to the right, and low lean thorn between,

And ye may hear a breech-bolt snick where never a man is seen.'

The Colonel's son has taken a horse, and a raw rough dun was he,

With the mouth of a bell and the heart of Hell and the head of a gallows tree.

The Colonel's son to the Fort has won, they bid him stay to eat—

Who rides at the tail of a Border thief, he sits not long at his meat.

He's up and away from Fort Bukloh as fast as he can fly,

Till he was aware of his father's mare with Kamal upon her back,

And when he could spy the white of her eye, he made the pistol crack.

He has fired once, he has fired twice, but the whistling ball went wide.

'Ye shoot like a soldier,' Kamal said. 'Show now if ye can ride.

It's up and over the Tongue of Jagai, as blown dust-devils go,

The dun he fled like a stag of ten, but the mare like a barren doe.

The dun he leaned against the bit and slugged his head above,

But the red mare played with the snaffle-bars, as a maiden plays with her glove.

There was rock to the left and rock to the right, and low lean
    thorn between,
And thrice he heard a breech-bait snick tho' never a man was
    seen.
They have ridden the low moon out of the sky, their hoofs drum
    up the dawn,
The dun he went like a wounded bull, but the mare like a new-
    roused fawn.
The dun he fell at ? water-course—in a woeful heap fell he,
And Kamal has turned the ted mare back, and pulled the rider
    free.
He has knocked the pistol out of his hand, small room was there
    to strive,
"Twas only by favour of mine,' quoth he, 'ye rode so long alive:
There was not a rock for twenty mile, there was not a clump of
    tree,
But covered a man of my own men with a rifle cocked On his
    knee.
If I had raised my bridle-hand, as I have held it low,
The little jackals that flee so fast were feasting all in a row.
If I had bowed my head on my breast, as I have held it high,
The kite that whistles above us now were gorged till she could not fly.'
Lightly answered the Colonel's son: 'Do good to bird and beast,
But count who come for the broken meats before thou makest feast.
If there should follow a thousand swords to carry my bones away,
Belike the price of a jackal's meal were more than a thief could
    pay.
They will feed their horse on the standing Crop, their men on the
    garnered grain,
The thatch of the byres will serve their fires when all the cattle
    are slain.
But if thou thinkest the price be fair,—thy brethren wait to sup,

The hound is kin to the jackal-spawn—howl, dog, and call them
   up!

And if thou thinkest the price be high, in steer and gear and stack,

Give me my father's mare again, and I'll fight my own way back!'

Kamal has gripped him by the hand and set him upon his feet.

'No talk shall be of dogs,' said he, 'when wolf and grey wolf meet.

May I eat dirt if thou hast hurt of me in deed or breath;

What dam of lances brought thee forth to jest at the dawn with
   Death?'

Lightly answered the Colonel's son: 'I hold by the blood of my
   clan:

Take up the mare for my father's gift—by God, she has carried
   a man!'

The red mare ran to the Colonel's son, and nuzzled against his
   breast;

'We be two strong men,' said Kamal then, 'but she loveth the
   younger best.

So shall she go with a lifter's dower, my turquoise-studded rein,

My broidered saddle and saddle-cloth, and silver stirrups twain.'

The Colonel's son a pistol drew and held it muzzle-end,

'Ye have taken the one from a foe,' said he; 'will ye take the mate,
   from a friend?'

'A gift for a gift,' said Kamal straight;'a limb for the risk of a limb.

Thy father has sent his son to me, I'll send my son to him!'

With that he whistled his only son, that dropped from a moun-
   tain-crest—

He trod the ling like a buck in spring, and he looked like a lance
   in rest.

'Now here is thy master,' Kamal said, 'who leads a troop of the
   Guides,

And thou must ride at his left side as shield on shoulder rides.

Till Death or I cut loose the tie, at camp and board and bed,

Thy life is his—thy fate it is to guard him with thy head.

So, thou must eat the White Queen's meat, and all her foes are thine,

And thou must harry thy father's hold for the peace of the Bor-
   der-line,

And thou must make a trooper tough and hack thy way to
   power—

Belike they will raise thee to Ressaldar when I am hanged in Pe-
shawur.'
They have looked each other between the eyes, and there they
have found no fault,
They have taken the Oath of the Brother-in-Blood on leavened
bread and salt:
They have taken the Oath of the Brother-in-Blood on fire and
fresh-cut sod,
On the hilt and the haft of the Khyber knife, and the Wondrous
"Names of God.

The Colonel's son he rides the mare and Kamal's boy the dun,
And two have come back to Fort Bukloh where there went forth
but one.
And when they drew to the Quarter-Guard, full twenty swords
flew clear–
There was not-a man but carried his feud with the blood of the
mountaineer.
'Ha' done! ha' done!' said the Colonel's son, 'Put up the steel at
your sides!

Last night ye had struck at a Border thief—to-night 'tis a man of
the Guides!'
Oh, East is East, and West is West, and never the twain shall meet,
Till Earth and Sky stand presently at God's great Judgment Seat;
But there is neither East nor West, Border, nor Breed nor Birth,
When two strong men stand face to face, though they come from the ends of
the earth!

RUDYARD KIPLING

THE HIGHWAYMAN

Part I

The wind was a torrent of darkness among the gusty trees, The
moon was a ghostly galleon tossed upon cloudy seas, The road
was a ribbon of moonlight over the purple moor,

And the highwayman came riding
      Riding—riding,

The highwayman came riding, up to the old inn-door.
He'd a French cocked-hat on his forehead, a bunch of lace at his
   chin,
A coat of claret velvet, and breeches of brown doe-skin,
They fitted with never a wrinkle; his boots were up to the thigh;
And he rode with a jewelled twinkle,
      His pistol butts a-twinkle,
His rapier hilt a-twinkle, under the jewelled sky.

Over the cobbles he clattered and clashed in the dark inn-yard;
And he tapped with his whip on the shutters, but all was
locked and barred;
He whistled a tune to the window, and who should be waiting
   there
But the landlord's black-eyed daughter,
      Bess, the landlord's daughter,
Plaiting a dark red love-knot into her long black hair.
And dark in the dark old inn-yard a stable wicket creaked,
Where Tim the ostler listened; his face was white and peaked;
His eyes were hollows of madness, his hair like mouldy hay,
But he loved the landlord's daughter—
      The landlord's red-lipped daughter—
Dumb as a dog he listened, and he heard the robber say—
'One kiss, my bonnie sweetheart, I'm after a prize to-night,
But I shall be back with the yellow gold before the morning light;
Yet, if they press me sharply, and harry me through the day,
Then look for me by moonlight,
      Watch for me by moonlight,
I'll come to thee by moonlight, though hell should bar the way:'

He rose upright in the stirrups; he scarce could reach her hand.

But she loosened her hair i' the casement! His bice burnt like a
  brand
As the black cascade of perfume came tumbling over his breast;
And he kissed the waves in the moonlight
          (Oh, sweet black waves in the moonlight);
Then he tugged at his rem in the moonlight, and galloped away
  to the west.

Part II

He did not come in the dawning; he did not come at noon;
And out o' the tawny sunset, before the rise o' the moon.
When the road was a gipsy's ribbon, looping the purple moor,
A red-coat troop came marching—
          Marching—marching,
King George's men came marching, up to the old inn-door.

They said no word to the landlord, they drank his ale instead,
But they gagged his daughter and bound her to the foot other
  narrow bed;
Two of them knelt at her casement, with muskets at their side!
There was death at every window;
And hell at one dark window;

For Bess could see, through her casement, the road that he would
  ride
They had tied her up to attention, with many a sniggering jest;
They had bound a musket beside herewith the barrel beneath her
  breast!
'Now keep good watch!' and they kissed her. She heard the dead
  man say—
'Look for me by moonlight;
    Watch for me by moonlight;
I'll come to thee by moonlight, though hell should bar the way!'

She twisted her hands behind her; but all the knots held good!
She writhed her hands till her fingers were wet with sweat, or
  blood.
They stretched and strained in the darkness, and the hours crawled

by like years,
Till, now, on the stroke of midnight.
Cold, on the stroke of midnight,
The tip of one finger touched it! The trigger at least was hers!

The tip of one finger touched it; she strove no more for the rest!
Up, she stood to attention, with the barrel beneath her breast,
She would not risk their hearing; she would not strive again;
For the road lay bare in the moonlight;
      Blank, and bare in the moonlight;
And the blood of her veins in the moonlight throbbed to her love's
   refrain,

Tlot-tlot; tlot-tlot! Had they heard it? The horse-hoofs ringing clear:
Tlot-tlot, tlot-tlot, in the distance! Were they deaf that they did not
   hear?
Down the ribbon of moonlight, over the brow of the hill.
The highwayman came riding,
      Riding, riding!
The red-coats looked to their priming! she stood up, straight and
   still!

Tlot-tlot, in the frosty silence! *Tlot-tlot,* in the echoing night!
Nearer he came and nearer! Her face was like a light!
Her eyes grew wide for a moment; she drew one last deep breath.
Then her finger moved in the moonlight,
Her musket shattered the moonlight,
Shattered her breast in the moonlight and warned him—with her
   death.

He turned; he spurred to the westward; he did not know who
   stood.
Bowed, with her head o'er the musket, drenched with her own
   red blood!
Not till the dawn he heard it, and slowly blanched to hear

How Bess, the landlord's daughter
The landlord's black-eyed daughter,
Had watched for her love in the moonlight, and died in the dark-
   ness there.

Back, he spurred like a madman, shrieking a curse to the sky,

With the white road smoking behind him and his rapier bran-
    dished high!
Blood-red were his spurs i' the golden noon; wine-red was his vel-
    vet coat;
When they shot him down on the highway,
            Down like a dog on the highway;
And he lay in his blood on the highway, with the bunch of lace at
    his throat.

And still of a winter's night, they say, when the wind is in the trees,
When the moon is a ghostly galleon tossed upon cloudy seas,
When the road is a ribbon of moonlight over the purple moor,
A highwayman comes riding
            Riding—riding,
A highwayman comes riding, up to the old inn-door.

Over the cobbles he clatters and clangs in the dark inn-yard;
And he taps with his whip on the shutters, but all is locked and
    barred;
He whistles a tune to the window, and who should be waiting
    there
But the landlord's black-eyed daughter,
            Bess, the landlord's daughter,
Plaiting a dark red love-knot into her long black hair.

                                                          ALFRED NOYES

THE TRAIN

Earth lies a violin to my bow:
And as I rush,
A thousand shapes of music grow
Out of the hush.

The leaping flame within me draws,
As it shoots lone,
Between each throbbing pause and pause.
Tone upon tone.

Strange orchestrated sounds unroll
From waiting woods;

And as my passion thrills the soul
Of solitudes,

1 hear a far-off rapture sweep
Me as 1 pass:
Loud waters dying in the deep,
Low sighs of grass;

Long echoes rolling to the ridge,
Or valley green;
The different notes of tunnel, bridge,
Or cleft ravine;

The fury of neglected stations—
A shrieking wind
Shrill with a million execrations
Of hag or fiend;

The murmurous silence when I stop,
Live with the noise
Of water drowsing drop by drop
Or human voice.

A little pause, and off I go ...
My simple art
Touches to music with my bow
Earth's silent heart.

ARMANDO MENEZES

HORATIUS

But the Consul's brow was sad,
    And the Consul's speech was low,
And darkly looked he at the wall,
    And darkly at the foe.
'Their van will be upon us
    Before the bridge goes down;
And if they once may win the bridge,
    What hope to save the town?'

Then out spake brave Horatius,
   The Captain of the Gate:
'To every man upon this earth
   Death cometh soon or late.
And bow can man die better
   Than facing fearful odds,
For the ashes of his fathers,
   And the temples of his Gods,

'And for the tender mother
   Who for dandled him to rest,
And for the wife who nurses
   His baby at her breast,
And for the holy maidens
   Who feed the eternal flame,
To save them from false Sextus
   That wrought the deed of shame?

'Hew down the bridge, Sir Consul,
   With all the speed ye may;
I, with two more to help me,
   Will hold the foe in play.
In yon strait path a thousand
   May well be stopped by three.
Now who will stand on either hand,
   And keep the bridge with me?'

Then out spake Spurius Lartius;
   A Ramnian proud was he:
'Lo, I will stand at thy right hand,
   And keep the bridge with thee.'
And out spake strong Herminius;
   Of Titian blood was he:
'I will abide on thy left side,
   And keep the bridge with thee.'

'Horatius,' quoth the Consul,

'As thou sayest, so let it be.'
And straight against that great array
   Forth went the dauntless Three.
For Romans in Rome's quarrel
   Spared neither land nor gold,
Nor son nor wife, nor limb nor life,
   In the brave days of old.

Meanwhile the Tuscan army,
   Right glorious to behold,
Came flashing back the noonday light,
Rank behind rank, like surges bright
   Of a broad sea of gold.
Four hundred trumpets sounded
   A peal of warlike glee,
As that great host, with measured tread,
And spears advanced, and ensigns spread,
Rolled slowly towards the bridge's head,
   Where stood the dauntless Three.

The Three stood calm and silent,
   And looked upon the foes,
And a great shout of laughter
   From all the vanguard rose:
And forth three chiefs came spurring
   Before that deep array;
To earth they sprang, their swords they drew,
And lifted high their shields, and flew
   To win the narrow way;

Then Ocnus of Falerii
   Rushed on the Roman Three;
And Lausulus of Urgo,
   The rover of the sea;
And Aruns of Volsinium,
   Who slew the great wild boar,
The great wild boar that had his den
Amidst the reeds of Cosa's fen,

And wasted fields; and slaughtered men,
    Along Albania's shore.
Herminius smote down Aruns:
    Lartius laid Ocnus low:
Right to the heart of Lausulus
    Horatius sent a blow.
'Lie there,' he cried, 'fell pirate!
    No more, aghast and pale,
From Ostia's walls the crowd shall mark
The track of thy destroying bark.
No more Campania's hinds shall fly
To woods and caverns when they spy
    Thy thrice accursed sail.'

But now no sound of laughter
    Was heard among the foes.
A wild and wrathful clamour
    From all the vanguard rose.
Six spears' lengths from the entrance
    Halted that deep array.
And for a space no man came forth
    To win the narrow way.

But all Etruria's noblest
    Felt their hearts sink to see
On the earth the bloody corpses.
    In the path the dauntless Three;
And from the ghastly entrance
    Where those bold Romans stood,
All shrank, like boys who unaware,
Ranging the woods to start a hare,
Come to the mouth of a dark lair
Where, growling low, a fierce old bear
    Lies amidst bones and blood.

Yet one man for one moment
    Strode out before the crowd;
Well known was he to all the Three,

And they gave him greeting loud.
'Now welcome, welcome, Sextus!
    Now welcome to thy home!
Why dost thou stay, and turn away?
    Here lies the road to Rome,'

Thrice looked he at the city;
    Thrice looked he at the dead;
And thrice came on in fury,
    And thrice turned back in dread:
And, white with fear and hatred.
    Scowled at the narrow way
Where wallowing in a pool of blood,
    The bravest Tuscans lay.

But meanwhile axe and lever
    Have manfully been plied;
And now the bridge hangs tottering
    Above the boiling tide.
'Come back, come back, Horatius!'
    Loud cried the Fathers all.
'Back, Lartius! back. Herminius!'
    Back, ere the ruin fall!"

Back darted Spurius Lartius;
    Herminius darted back:
And, as they passed, beneath their feet
    They felt the timbers crack.
But when they turned their faces.
    And on the farther shore
Saw brave Horatius stand alone.
    They would have crossed once more.

But with a crash like thunder
    Fell every loosened beam.
And. like a dam, the mighty wreck
    Lay right athwart the stream:
And a long shout of triumph

Rose from the walls of Rome.
As to the highest turret-tops
   Was splashed the yellow foam.

Alone stood brave Horatius,
   But constant still in mind;
Thrice thirty thousand foes before,
   And the broad flood behind.
'Down with him!' cried false Sextus,
   'With a smile on his pale face.
'Now yield thee,' cried Lars Porsena,
   'Now yield thee to our grace.'

Round turned he, as not deigning
   Those craven ranks to see;
Nought spake he to Lars Porsena,
   To Sextus nought spake he;
But he saw on Palatinus
   The white porch of his home;
And he spake to the noble river
   That rolls by the towers of Rome.

'Oh, Tiber! father Tiber!
   To whom the Romans pray,
A Roman's life, a Roman's arms,
   Take thou in charge this day!'
So he spake, and speaking sheathed
   The good sword by his side,
And with his harness on his back,
   Plunged headlong in the tide.

No sound of joy or sorrow
   Was heard from either bank;
But friends and foes in dumb surprise.
With parted lips and straining eyes,
   Stood gazing where he sank:
And when above the surges
   They saw his crest appear,

All Rome sent forth a rapturous cry.
And even the ranks of Tuscany
  Could scarce forbear to cheer.

But fiercely ran the current
  Swollen high by months of rain:
And fast his blood was flowing;
  And he was sore in pain,
And heavy with his armour,
  And spent with changing blows:
And oft they thought him sinking,
  But still again he rose.

Never, I ween, did swimmer,
  In such an evil case,
Struggle through such a raging flood
  Safe to the landing place:
But his limbs were borne up bravely
  By the brave heart within,
And our good father Tiber
  Bare bravely up his chin.

'Curse on him!' quoth false Sextus;
  'Will not the villain drown?
But for this stay, ere close of day
  We should have sacked the town!'
'Heaven help him!' quoth Lars Porsena,
  'And bring him safe to shore;
For such a gallant feat of arms
  Was never seen before.'

And now he feels the bottom:
  Now on dry earth he stands;
Now round him throng the Fathers
  To press his gory hands;
And now, with shouts and clapping,
  And noise of weeping loud,
He enters through the River-Gate,
  Borne by the joyous crowd.

They gave him of the corn-land,
　That, was of public right,
As much as two strong oxen
　Could plough from morn till night;
And they made a molten image.
　And set it up on high,
And there it stands unto this day
　To witness if I lie.

　　　　　Lord Macaulay

7. PATRIOTISM

TO INDIA—MY NATIVE LAND

My country! in thy day of glory past
A beauteous halo circled round thy brow,
And worshipped as a deity thou wast.
Where is that glory, where that reverence now?
Thy eagle pinion is chained down at last,
And grovelling in the lowly dust art thou;
Thy minstrel hath no wreath to weave for thee
Save the sad story of thy misery!
Well—let me dive into the depths of time,
And bring from out the ages that have rolled
A few small fragments of those wrecks sublime,
Which human eyes may never more behold;
And let the guerdon of my labour be
My fallen country! one kind wish from thee!

Henry Louis Vivian Derozio

THE WARRIOR'S RETURN

When the Maharaja Jeswunt Sing, being defeated by Aurungzeb
fled for refuge to his own capital, his wife, with Spartan haughti-
ness, refused him admittance, saying, 'This man is impostor, for
the brave never return with dishonour. My husband sleeps on the
field of battle.'

Heard ye that lofty pealing sound
   Upon the balmy air,
Th' exulting shout that best proclaims
   The deeds which heroes dare?

In triumph blow their trumpets proud,
   The clouds repeat their voice;

Go, greet the laurell'd victors home,
    And bid our realms rejoice.

Let poets tune their golden harps,
    Let maidens wear their smile,
And young and old their cares lay by,
    And cease to mourn awhile.

What! hear st thou not their joyous din?
    Behold, above the vale,
Their haughty plumes and ensigns red
    Are flutt'ring in the gale;

And helmets cleft, and canvas torn,
    Proclaim the fighting done;
And neighing steeds, and bloody spears,
    Announce the battle won.

Alas! the vision mocks my sight;
    I see no gallant throng,
No trophies meet my longing eyes;
    Bid cease the joyous song.

That recreant slave is not my lord;
    Ne'er thus the brave return;
Go, bid the city-gates be barr'd,
    And leave me lone to mourn.,

I know him not. I never knew
    A low ignoble love;
My warrior sleeps upon the moor,
    His soul hath soar'd above.

Upon the battle-field he lies
    His garments stain'd with gore;
With sword in hand prepared he sleeps
    To fight the battle o'er.

His shiver'd shield, his broken spear
    Around him scatter'd lie;
The iron-breasted Moslems shook
    To see my hero die.

Where helmets rang, where sabres smote,
    He found his gory bed;
Join, mourners, join, and loudly raise
    The requiem of the dead.

Expel yon vile impostor hence;
    I will not trust his tale;
Our warriors on the crimson field
    Their chieftain's loss bewail.

The mountain torrent rushing down
    Can ne'er its course retrace.
And souls that speed on glory's path
    Must ever onward press:

Aye. onward press—to bleed and die,
    Triumphant still in death: Impostor,
hence! in other lands
    Go draw thy coward breath.

                    SHOSHEE CHUNDER DUTT

WHERE THE MIND IS WITHOUT FEAR

Where the mind is without fear and the head is held high;
    Where knowledge is free;
    Where the world has not been broken up into fragments
by narrow domestic walls;
    Where words come out from the depth of truth;
    Where tireless striving stretches its arms towards perfection;
    Where the clear stream of reason has not lost its way into the
        dreary desert sand of dead habit;
    Where the mind is led forward by thee into ever-widening
        thought and action—
    Into that heaven of freedom, my Father, let my country awake.

                    RABINDRANATH TAGORE

THE PATRIOT

I am standing for peace and non-violence.
Why world is fighting fighting
Why all people of world
Are not following Mahatma Gandhi,
I am simply not understanding.
Ancient Indian Wisdom is 100% correct.
I should say even 200% correct.
But modern generation is neglecting—
Too much going for fashion and foreign thing.

Other day I'm reading in newspaper
(Every day I'm reading Times of India
To improve my English Language)
How one goonda fellow
Throw stone at Indirabehn.
Must be student unrest fellow, I am thinking.
Friends, Romans, Countrymen, I am saying
   (to myself)
Lend me the ears. Everything is coming—
Regeneration, Remuneration, Contraception.
Be patiently, brothers and sisters.

You want one glass lassi?
Very good for digestion.
With little salt lovely drink,
Better than wine;
Not that I am ever tasting the wine.
I'm the total teetotaller, completely total.
But I say
Wine is for the drunkards only.

What you think of prospects of world peace?
Pakistan behaving like this,
China behaving like that,
It is making me very sad, I am telling you.
Really, most harassing me.

All men are brothers, no?
In India also
Gujaraties, Maharashtrians, Hindiwallahs
All brothers—
Though some are having funny habits.
Still, you tolerate me, I tolerate you,
One day Ram Rajya is surely coming.

You are going?
But you will visit again
Any time, any day,
I am not believing in ceremony.
Always I am enjoying your company.

NISSIM EZEKIEL

PATRIOTISM

Breathes there the man with soul so dead,
Who never to himself hath said,
   'This is my own, my native land!'
Whose heart hath ne'er within him burn'd,
As home his footsteps he hath turn'd,
   From wandering on a foreign strand!
If such there breathe, go mark him well;
For him no Minstrel raptures swell;
High though his titles, proud his name,
Boundless his wealth as wish can claim;
Despite those titles, power, and pelf,
The wretch, concentred all in self,
Living, shall forfeit fair renown,
And, doubly dying, shall go down
To the vile dust from whence he sprung,
Unwept, unhonour'd, and unsung.

SIR WALTER SCOTT

THE PATRIOT
AN OLD STORY

I

It was roses, roses, all the way,
With myrtle mixed in my path like mad;
The house-roofs seemed to heave and sway,
The church-spires flamed, such flags they had,
A year ago on this very day.

II

The air broke into a mist with bells,
The old walls rocked with the crowd and cries.
Had I said, 'Good folk, mere noise repels—
But give me your sun from yonder skies!'
They had answered, 'And afterward, what else?'

III

Alack, it was I who leaped at the sun
To give it my loving friends to keep!
Naught man could do, have I left undone:
And you see my harvest, what 1 reap
This very day, now a year is run.

IV

There's nobody on the house-tops now—
Just a palsied few at the windows set;
For the best of the sight is, all allow,
At the Shambles' Gate—or, better yet,
By the very scaffold's foot, I trow.

V

I go in the rain; and, more than needs,
A rope cuts both my wrists behind;.
And I think, by the feel, my forehead bleeds,

For they fling, whoever has a mind,
Stones at me for my year's misdeeds.

VI

Thus I entered, and thus I go!
In triumphs, people have dropped down dead
'Paid by the world, what dost thou owe
Me?' God might question; now instead,
'Tis God shall repay: 1 am safer so.

ROBERT BROWNING

IRELAND, IRELAND

Down thy valleys, Ireland, Ireland,
    Down thy valleys green and sad,
Still thy spirit wanders wailing,
    Wanders wailing, wanders mad.

Long ago that anguish took thee,
    Ireland, Ireland, green and fair,
Spoilers strong in darkness took thee,
    Broke thy heart and left thee there.

Down thy valleys, Ireland, Ireland,
    Still thy spirit wanders mad;
All too late they love that wronged thee,
    Ireland, Ireland, green and sad.

SIR HENRY NEWBOLT

EASTER 1916

I have met them at close of day
Coming with vivid faces
From counter or desk among grey
Eighteenth-century houses.
I have passed with a nod of the head

Or polite meaningless words,
Or have lingered awhile and said
Polite meaningless words.
And thought before I had done
Of a mocking tale or a gibe
To please a companion
Around the fire at the club,
Being certain that they and I
But lived where motley is worn:
All changed, changed utterly:
A terrible beauty is born.

That woman's days were spent
In ignorant good-will,
Her nights in argument
Until her voice grew shrill.
What voice more sweet than hers
When, young and beautiful.
She rode to harriers?
This man had kept a school
And rode our winged horse:
This other his helper and friend
Was coming into his force
He might have won fame in the end,
So sensitive his nature seemed.
So daring and sweet his thought.
This other man I had dreamed
A drunken, vainglorious lout.
He had done most bitter wrong
To some who are near my heart,
Yet I number him in the song;
He, too, has resigned his part
In the casual comedy;
He, too, has been changed in his turn,
Transformed utterly:
A terrible beauty is born.

Hearts with one purpose alone
Through summer and winter seem

Enchanted to a stone
To trouble the living stream.
The horse that comes from the road.
The rider, the birds that range
From cloud to tumbling cloud,
Minute by minute they change;
A shadow of cloud on the stream
Changes minute by minute;
A horse-hoof slides on the brim,
And a horse plashes within it;
The long-legged moor-hens dive,
And hens to moor-cocks call;
Minute by minute they live:
The stone's in the midst of all.

Too long a sacrifice
Can make a stone of the heart.
O when may it suffice?
That is Heaven's part, our part
To murmur name upon name,
As a mother names her child
When sleep at last has come
On limbs that had run wild.
What is it but nightfall?
No, no, not night but death;
Was it needless death after all?
For England may keep faith
For all that is done and said.
We know their dream; enough
To know they dreamed and are dead;

And what if excess of love
Bewildered them till they died?
I write it out in a verse—
MacDonagh and MacBride
And Connolly and Pearse
Now and in time to be,

Wherever green is worn.
Are changed, changed utterly:
A terrible beauty is born.

WILLIAM BUTLER YEATS

THE SOLDIER

If I should die, think only this of me:
  That there's some corner of a foreign field
That is for ever England. There shall be
  In that rich earth a richer dust concealed;
A dust whom England bore, shaped, made aware,
  Gave, once, her flowers to love, her ways to roam,
A body of England's, breathing English air,
  Washed by the rivers, blest by suns of home.

And think, this heart, all evil shed away,
  A pulse in the eternal mind, no less
    Gives somewhere back the thoughts by England given;
Her sights and sounds; dreams happy as her day;
  And laughter, learnt of friends; and gentleness,
    In hearts at peace, under an English heaven.

RUPERT BROOKE

8. DEATH AND HEROISM

DEATH THE LEVELLER

The glories of our blood and state
  Are shadows, not substantial things;
There is no armour against fate;
  Death lays his icy hand on kings:
      Sceptre and Crown
      Must tumble down,
And in the dust be equal made
With the poor crooked scythe and spade.

Some men with swords may reap the field,
  And plant fresh laurels where they kill:
But their strong nerves at last must yield;
  They tame but one another still:
      Early or late
      They stoop to fate.
And must give up their murmuring breath
When they, pale captives, creep to death.

The garlands wither on your brow;
  Then boast no more your mighty deeds;
Upon Death's purple altar now
  See where the victor-victim bleeds:
      Your heads must come
      To the cold tomb;
Only the actions of the just
Smell sweet, and blossom in their dust.

                          JAMES SHIRLEY

ON THE DEATH OF MR ROBERT LEVET
A PRACTISER IN PHYSIC

Condemned to Hope's delusive mine,
   As on we toil from day to day,
By sudden blasts or slow decline
   Our social comforts drop away.

Well tried through many a varying year,
   See Levet to the grave descend;
Officious, innocent, sincere.
   Of every friendless name the friend.

Yet still he fills affection's eye,
   Obscurely wise and coarsely kind;
Nor, lettered Arrogance, deny
   Thy praise to merit unrefined.

When fainting nature called for aid,
   And hovering death prepared the blow,
His vigorous remedy displayed
   The power of art without the show.

In Misery's darkest cavern known.
   His useful care was ever nigh,
Where hopeless Anguish poured his groan
   And lonely Want retired to die.

No summons mocked by chill delay,
   No petty gain disdained by pride;
The modest wants of every day
   The toil of every day supplied.

His virtues walked their narrow round,
   Nor made a pause, nor left a void;
And sure the Eternal Master found
   The single talent well employed.

The busy day, the peaceful night,
   Unfelt, uncounted, glided by;
His frame was firm—his powers were bright.
   Though now his eightieth year was nigh.

Then with no fiery throbbing pain,
   No cold gradations of decay,
Death broke at once the vital chain,
   And freed his soul the nearest way.

SAMUEL JOHNSON

THE DYING GLADIATOR

I see before me the Gladiator lie:
He leans upon his hand—his manly brow
Consents to death, but conquers agony,
And his droop'd head sinks gradually low—
And through his side the last drops, ebbing slow
From the red gash, fall heavy, one by one,
Like the first of a thunder-shower; and now
The arena swims around him—he is gone,
Ere ceased the inhuman shout which hailed the
     wretch who won.

He heard it, but he heeded not—his eyes
Were with his heart, and that was far away;
He reck'd not of the life he lost, nor prize,
But where his rude hut by the Danube lay,
There were his young barbarians all at play,
There was their Dacian mother—he, their sire,
Butcher'd to make a Roman holiday—
All this rushed with his blood—Shall he expire
And unavenged?—Arise! ye Goths, and glut your ire

GEORGE GORDON NOEL, LORD BYRON

FROM 'THE PASSING OF ARTHUR'

So all day long the noise of battle roll'd
Among the mountains by the winter sea;
Until King Arthur's Table, man by man,
Had fall'n in Lyonnesse about their lord,
King Arthur. Then, because his wound was deep,
The bold Sir Bedivere uplifted him,
Sir Bedivere, the last of all his knights,
And bore him to a chapel nigh the field,
A broken chancel with a broken cross,
That stood on a dark strait of barren land.
On one side lay the Ocean, and on one
Lay a great water, and the moon was full.

   Then spake King Arthur to Sir Bedivere;
'The sequel of to-day unsolders all
The goodliest fellowship of famous knights
Whereof this world holds record. Such a sleep
They sleep—the men I loved. I think that we
Shall never more, at any future time,
Delight our souls with talk of knightly deeds,
Walking about the gardens and the halls
Of Camelot, as in the days that were.
I perish by this people which I made,—
Tho' Merlin sware that I should come again
To rule once more; but, let what will be, be,
I am so deeply smitten thro' the helm
That without help I cannot last till morn.
Thou therefore take my brand Excalibur,
Which was my pride: for thou rememberest how
In those old days, one summer noon, an arm
Rose up from out the bosom of the lake,
Clothed in white samite, mystic, wonderful,
Holding the sword—and how I row'd across
And took it, and have worn it, like a king:
And, wheresoever I am sung or told
In aftertime, this also shall be known:
But now delay not: take Excalibur,

And fling him far into the middle mere:
Watch what thou seest, and lightly bring me word.'

***

   Then quickly rose Sir Bedivere, and ran,
And, leaping down the ridges lightly, plunged
Among the bulrush beds, and clutch'd the sword,
And strongly wheel'd and threw it. The great brand
Made lightnings in the splendour of the moon,
And flashing round and round, and whirl'd in an arch,
Shot like a streamer of the northern morn,
Seen where the moving isles of winter shock
By night, with noises of the northern sea.
So flash'd and fell the brand Excalibur:
But ere he dipt the surface, rose an arm
Clothed in white samite, mystic, wonderful,
And caught him by the hilt, and brandish'd him
Three times, and drew him under in the mere.
And lightly went the other to the King.

***

   And answer made King Arthur, breathing hard:
'My end draws nigh; 'tis time that I were gone.
Make broad thy shoulders to receive my weight,
And bear me to the margin; yet I fear
My wound hath taken cold, and I shall die.'

   So saying, from the pavement he half rose,
Slowly, with pain, reclining on his arm,
And looking wistfully with wide blue eyes
As in a picture. Him Sir Bedivere
Remorsefully regarded thro' his tears,
And would have spoken, but he found not words;
Then took with care, and kneeling on one knee,
O'er both his shoulders drew the languid hands,
And rising bore him thro' the place of tombs.

But, as he walked, King Arthur panted hard,
Like one that feels a nightmare on his bed
When all the house is mute. So sigh'd the King,
Muttering and murmuring at his ear, 'Quick, quick!
I fear it is too late, and I shall die.'
But the other swiftly strode from ridge to ridge,
Clothed with his breath, and looking, as he walk'd,
Larger than human on the frozen hills.
He heard the deep behind him, and a cry
Before. His own thought drove him like a goad.
Dry clash'd his harness in the icy caves
And barren chasms, and all to left and right
The bare black cliff clang'd round him, as he based
His feet on juts of slippery crag that rang
Sharp-smitten with the dint of armed heels—
And on a sudden, lo! the level lake,
And the long glories of the winter moon.

Then saw they how there hove a dusky barge,
Dark as a funeral scarf from stem to stern,
Beneath them; and descending they were ware
That all the decks were dense with stately forms,
Black-stoled, black-hooded, like a dream—by these
Three Queens with crowns of gold—and from them rose
A cry that shiver'd to the tingling stars,
And, as it were one voice, an agony
Of lamentation, like a wind that shrills
All night in a waste land, where no one comes,
Or hath come, since the making of the world.

Then murmur'd Arthur, 'Place me in the barge.'
So to the barge they came. There those three Queens
Put forth their hands, and took the King, and wept.
But she, that rose the tallest of them all
And fairest laid his head upon her lap,
And loosed the shatter'd casque, and chafed his hands
And call'd him by his name, complaining-loud
And dropping bitter tears against his brow

Striped with dark blood: for all his face was white
And colourless, and like the wither'd moon
Smote by the fresh beam of the springing east;
And all his greaves and cuisses dash'd with drops
Of onset; and the light and lustrous curls—
That made his forehead like a rising sun
High from the dais-throne—were parch'd with dust;
Or, clotted into points and hanging loose,
Mix'd with the knightly growth that fringed his lips.
So like a shatter'd column lay the King;
Not like that Arthur who, with lance in rest,
From spur to plume a star of tournament,
Shot thro' the lists at Camelot, and charged
Before the eyes of ladies and of kings.

Then loudly cried the bold Sir Bedivere:
'Ah! my Lord Arthur, whither shall I go?
Where shall I hide my forehead and my eyes?
For now I see the true old times are dead.
When every morning brought a noble chance,
And every chance brought out a noble knight.
Such times have been not since the light that led
The holy Elders with the gift of myrrh.
But now the whole Round Table is dissolved
Which was an image of the mighty world,
And I, the last, go forth companionless.
And the days darken round me, and the years,
Among new men. strange faces, other minds.'

And slowly answer'd Arthur from the barge:
'The old order changeth. yielding place to new,
And God fulfils himself in many ways,
Lest one good custom should corrupt the world.
Comfort thyself: what comfort is in me?
I have lived my life, and that which I have done
May He within himself make pure! but thou,
If thou shouldst never see my face again,
Pray for my soul. More things are wrought by prayer

Than this world dreams of. Wheretore, let thy voice
Rise like a fountain for me night and day.
For what are men better than sheep or goats
That nourish a blind life within the brain,
If, knowing God, they lift not hands of prayer
Both for themselves and those who call them friend?
For so the whole round earth is every way
Bound by gold chains about the feet of God.
But now farewell. I am going a long way
With these thou seest–if indeed I go—
(For all my mind is clouded with a doubt)—
To the island-valley of Avilion;
Where falls not hail, or rain, or any snow,
Nor ever wind blows loudly; but it lies
Deep-meadow'd, happy, fair with orchard lawns
And bowery hollows crown'd with summer sea,
Where I will heal me of my grievous wound.'

　　So said he, and the barge with oar and sail
Moved from the brink, like some full-breasted swan
That, fluting a wild carol ere her death,
Ruffles her pure cold plume, and takes the flood
With swarthy webs. Long stood Sir Bedivere
Revolving many memories, till the hull
Look'd one black dot against the verge of dawn,
And on the mere the wailing died away.

　　But when that moan had past for evermore,
The stillness of the dead world's winter dawn
Amazed him, and he groan'd, 'The King is gone.'
And therewithal came on him the weird rhyme,
'From the great deep to the great deep he goes.'

　　Whereat he slowly turn'd and slowly clomb
The last hard footstep of that iron crag;
Thence mark'd the black hull moving yet, and cried,
'He passes to be King among the dead,
And after healing of his grievous wound

He comes again; but—if he comes no more—
O me, be yon dark Queens in yon black boat,
Who shriek'd and wail'd, the three whereat we gazed
On that high day, when, clothed with living light,
They stood before his throne in silence, friends
Of Arthur, who should help him at his need?'

    Then from the dawn it seem'd there came, but faint
As from beyond the limit of the world,
Like the last echo born of a great cry,
Sounds, as if some fair city were one voice
Around a king returning from his wars.

    Thereat once more he moved about, and clomb
Ev'n to the highest he could climb, and saw,
Straining his eyes beneath an arch of hand,
Or thought he saw, the speck that bare the King,
Down that long water opening on the deep
Somewhere far off, pass on and on, and go
From less to less and vanish into light.
And the new sun rose bringing the new year.

ALFRED, LORD TENNYSON

AN IRISH AIRMAN FORESEES HIS DEATH

I know that I shall meet my fate
Somewhere among the clouds above;
Those that I fight I do not hate,
Those that I guard I do not love;
My country is Kiltartan Cross,
My countrymen Kiltartan's poor,
No likely end could bring them loss
Or leave them happier than before

Nor law, nor duty bade me fight,
Nor public men, nor cheering crowds,
A lonely impulse of delight

Drove to this tumult in the clouds,
I balanced all, brought all to mind,
The years to come seemed waste of breath,
A waste of breath the years behind
In balance with this life, this death,

WILLIAM BUTLER YEATS

AURUNGZEB AT HIS FATHER'S BIER

The monarch lay upon his bier;
   Censers were burning low,
As through the lofty arches streamed
   The setting, sun's red glow.
Still grasped he in his hand the blade
   Which well-fought fields had won,
And Aurungzeb beside him knelt,
   Usurper proud and son.

Remorse had stricken his false heart
   And quenched his wonted fire;
With gloomy brow and look intent
   He gazed upon his sire:

Can tyrant death make *him* afraid?
   Hot tears burst from his eyes,
As thus his grief found vent in words
   To the warrior-train's surprise.

'Father, thou wert the goodliest king
   That e'er the sceptre swayed;
How could I then lift up my arm
   Against thee undismayed?
How could I send thee here to pine,
   Usurp the peacock-throne;
Oh! had I perished in the womb,
   That deed were left undone.

See, all is changed that was estranged,
    Awake, my sire, my king,
See, soldiers in their war array
    Thy son in fetters bring!
Thy rebel son who will abide
    Thy word whate'er it be,
And fearless meet the rack or steel,
    Rise up once more and see!

Thou wilt not hear—thou wilt not speak
    It is the last long sleep.—
And am I not a king myself?
    What mean these stirrings deep?
Oh! foolish eyes, what means this rheum?
    I will not call them tears;
My heart which nothing e'er could daunt
    Is faint with boding fears.

The past appears! a checker'd field
    Of guilt and shame and war,
What evil influence ruled my birth,
    What swart malignant star?
Why did I barter peace of mind
    For royal pomp and state?
Mad for the baleful meteor's gleam,
    With worldly joys elate.

Remembered voices speak my name
    And call me parricide,
The murdered Dara beckons me—
    He was thy joy and pride:
And thus I fling the dear-bought crown,
    But whither can I fly?
The awful thought still follows me
    That even kings will die.'

                    HUR CHUNDER DUTT

ON KILLING A TREE

It takes much time to kill a tree,
Not a simple jab of the knife
Will do it. It has grown
Slowly consuming the earth,
Rising Out of it, feeding
Upon its crust, absorbing
Years of sunlight, air, water,
And out of its leperous hide
Sprouting leaves.

So hack and chop
But this alone wont do it.
Not so much pain will do it.
The bleeding bark will heal
And from close to the ground
Will rise curled green twigs,
Miniature boughs
Which if unchecked will expand again
To former size.

No,
The root is to be pulled out—
Out of the anchoring earth;
It is to be roped, tied,
And pulled out—snapped out
Or pulled out entirely.
Out from the earth-cave,
And the strength of the tree exposed
The source, white and wet,
The most sensitive, hidden
For years inside the earth.
Then the matter
Of scorching and choking

In sun and air,
Browning, hardening.
Twisting, withering,

And then it is done.

GIEVE PATEL

O CAPTAIN! MY CAPTAIN!

O Captain! my Captain! our fearful trip is done,
The ship has weather'd every rack, the prize we sought is won.
The port is near, the bells I hear, the people all exulting,
While follow eyes the steady keel, the vessel grim and daring;
   But O heart! heart! heart!
     O the bleeding drops of red!
       Where on the deck my Captain lies,
         Fallen cold and dead.
O Captain! my Captain! rise up and hear the bells;
Rise up—for you the flag is flung—for you the bugle trills,
For you bouquets and ribbon'd wreaths—for you the shores crowd-
  ing,
For you they call, the swaying mass, their eager faces turning;
   Here, Captain! dear father!
     This arm beneath your head!
       It is some dream that on the deck
         You've fallen cold and dead.
My Captain does not answer, his lips are pale and still,
My father does not feel my arm, he has no pulse nor will;
The ship is anchor'd safe and sound, its voyage closed and done.
From fearful trip the victor ship comes in with object won;
   Exult, O shores! and ring, O bells!
     But I, with mournful tread,
       Walk the deck my Captain lies,
         Fallen cold and dead.

WALT WHITMAN

9. HISTORICAL CHARACTERS, SCENES AND EVENTS

SOME INDIAN USES OF HISTORY ON A RAINY DAY

1

Madras,
             1965, and rain.
Head clerks from city banks
curse, batter, elbow
in vain the patchwork gangs
of coolies in their scramble
for the single seat in
the seventh bus:

they tell each other how
Old King Harsha's men
beat soft gongs
to stand a crowd of ten
thousand monks
in a queue, to give them
and the single visiting Chinaman
a hundred pieces of gold,
a pearl, and a length of cloth;

so, miss another bus, the eighth,
and begin to walk, for King Harsha's
monks had nothing but their own two feet.

2

Fulbright Indians, tiepins of ivory,
colour cameras for eyes, stand every July
in Egypt among camels,

faces pressed against the past
as against museum glass,

tongue tasting dust,
amazed at pyramidfuls
of mummies swathed in millennia
of Calicut muslin.

3

1935. Professor of Sanskrit
on cultural exchange;
               passing through; lost
in Berlin rain: reduced
to a literal, turbanned child,
spelling German signs on door, bus, and shop,
trying to guess *go* from *stop*;

                                 desperate

for a way of telling apart
a familiar street from a strange,
or east
from west at night,
the brown dog that barks
from the brown dog that doesn't,

memorizing a foreign paradigm
of lanterns, landmarks,
a gothic lotus on the iron gate;

suddenly comes home
in English, gesture, and Sanskrit,
assimilating

                              the swastika

on the neighbour's arm
in that roaring bus from a grey
nowhere to a green.

A.K. RAMANUJAN

AFTER BLENHEIM

It was a summer evening,
  Old Kaspar's work was done,
And he before his cottage door

Was sitting in the sun;
And by him sported on the green
His little grandchild Wilhelmine.
She saw her brother Peterkin
    Roll something large and round,
Which he beside the rivulet
    In playing there had found;
He came to ask what he had found
That was so large and smooth and round.

Old Kaspar took it from the boy
    Who stood expectant by;
And then the old man shook his head,
    And with a natural sigh
'Tis some poor fellow's skull,' said he,
'Who fell in the great victory.'

'I find them in the garden,
    For there's many here about;
And often when I go to plough
    The ploughshare turns them out.
For many thousand men,' said he,
'Were slain in that great victory.'

'Now tell us what 'twas all about,'
    Young Peterkin he cries;
And little Wilhelmine looks up
    With wonder-waiting eyes;
'Now tell us all about the war,
And what they fought each other for.'

'It was the English,' Kaspar cried,
    'Who put the French to rout;
But what they fought each other for
    I could not well make out.
But everybody said,' quoth he,
'That 'twas a famous victory.'

My father lived at Blenheim then,
    Yon little stream hard by;
They burnt his dwelling to the ground,
    And he was forced to fly:
So with his wife and child he fled.
Nor had he where to rest his head.
With fire and sword the country round
    Was wasted far and wide,
And many a childing mother then
    And newborn baby died:
But things like that, you know, must be
At every famous victory.

They say it was a shocking sight
    After the field was won;
For many thousand bodies here
    Lay rotting in the sun:
But things like that, you know, must be
After a famous victory.

Great praise the Duke of Marlbro' won
    And our good Prince Eugene;'
'Why, 'twas a very wicked thing!'
    Said little Wilhelmine.
'Nay... nay... my little girl,' quoth he,
it was a famous victory.'

'And everybody praised the Duke
    Who this great fight did win.'
'But what good came of it at last?'
    Quoth little Peterkin.
'Why that I cannot tell,' said he,
'But 'twas a famous victory.'

ROBERT SOUTHEY

THE BURIAL OF SIR JOHN MOORE AT CORUNNA

Not a drum was heard, not a funeral note,
    As his corse to the rampart we hurried;

Not a soldier discharged his farewell shot
   O'er the grave where our hero we buried.

We buried him darkly at dead of night,
   The sods with our bayonets turning,
By the struggling moonbeam's misty light
   And the lanthorn dimly burning;

No useless coffin enclosed his breast,
   Not in sheet or in shroud we wound him;
But he lay like a warrior taking his rest,
   With his martial cloak around him.

Few and short were the prayers we said,
   And we spoke not a word of sorrow;
But we steadfastly gazed on the face that was dead.
   And we bitterly thought of the morrow.

We thought, as we hollowed his narrow bed
   And smoothed down his lonely pillow,
That the foe and the stranger would tread o'er his head,
   And we far away on the billow!

Lightly they'll talk of the spirit that's gone,
   And o'er his cold ashes upbraid him—
But little he'll reck, if they let him sleep on
   In the grave where a Briton has laid him.

But half of our heavy task was done
   When the clock struck the hour for retiring;
And we heard the distant and random gun,
   That the foe was sullenly firing.

Slowly and sadly we laid him down,
   From the field of his fame fresh and gory;
We carved not a line, and we raised not a stone,
   But we left him alone with his glory.

CHARLES WOLFE

PAUL REVERE'S RIDE

Listen, my children, and you shall hear
Of the midnight ride of Paul Revere,
On the eighteenth of April, in Seventy-five;
Hardly a man is now alive
Who remembers that famous day and year.

He said to his friend. 'If the British march
By land or sea from the town tonight,
Hang a lantern aloft in the belfry arch
Of the North Church tower as a signal light,—
One, if by land, and two, if by Sea;
And I on the opposite shore will be,
Ready to ride and spread the alarm
Through every Middlesex village and farm,
For the country-folk to be up and to arm.'

Then he said, 'Good-night!' and with muffled oar
Silently he rowed to the Charlestown shore,
Just as the moon rose over the bay,
Where swinging wide at her moorings lay
The Somerset, British man-of-war;
A phantom ship, with each mast and spar
Across the moon like a prison bar,
And a huge black hulk, that was magnified
By its own reflection in the tide.

Meanwhile, his friend, through alley and street,
Wanders and watches with eager ears,
Till in the silence around him he hears
The muster of men at the barrack door,
The sound of arms, and the tramp of feet,
And the measured tread of the grenadiers,
Marching down to their boats on the shore.

Then he climbed to the tower of the church,
Up the wooden stairs, with stealthy tread,
To the belfry-chamber overhead,

And startled the pigeons from their perch
On the sombre rafters, that round him made
Masses and moving shapes of shade—
Up the trembling ladder, steep and tall,
To the highest window in the wall.
Where he paused to listen and look down
A moment on the roofs of the town,
And the moonlight flowing over all.

Beneath, in the churchyard lay the dead,
In their night-encampment on the hill,
Wrapped in silence so deep and still
That he could hear, like the sentinel's tread.
The watchful night-wind, as it went
Creeping along from tent to tent,
And seeming to whisper, 'All is well!'
A moment only he feels the spell
Of the place and the hour, and the secret dread
Of the lonely belfry and the dead,
For suddenly all his thoughts are bent
On a shadowy something far away,
Where the river widens to meet the bay—
A line of black that bends and floats
On the rising tide, like a bride of boats.

Meanwhile, impatient to mount and ride,
Booted and spurred, with a heavy stride
On the opposite shore walked Paul Revere.
Now he patted his horse's side,
Now gazed at the landscape far and near,
Then, impetuous, stamped the earth
And turned and tightened his saddle-girth,
But mostly he watched with eager search
The belfry tower of the Old North Church,
As it rose above the graves on the hill,
Lonely and spectral and sombre and still.
And lo! as he looks, on the belfry's height
A glimmer, and then a gleam of light!
He springs to the saddle, the bridle he turns,

But lingers and gazes, till full on his sight
A second lamp in the belfry burns!

A hurry of hoofs in a village street,
A shape in the moonlight, a bulk in the dark,
And beneath from the pebbles, in passing, a spark
Struck out by a steed flying fearless and fleet,
That was all! And yet, through the gloom and the light
The fate of a nation was riding that night,
And the spark struck out by that steed, in his flight,
Kindled the land into flame with its heat.
He has left the village and mounted the steep,
And beneath him, tranquil and broad and deep.
Is the Mystic, meeting the ocean tides,
And under the alders that skirt its edge,
Now soft on the sand, now loud on the ledge,
Is heard the tramp of his steed as he rides.

It was one by the village clock
When he galloped into Lexington.
He saw the gilded weathercock
Swim in the moonlight as he passed,
And the meeting-house windows, blank and bare.
Gaze at him with a spectral glare,
As if they already stood aghast
At the bloody work they would look upon.

It was two by the village clock
When he came to the bridge in Concord town.
He heard the bleating of the flock,
And the twitter of birds among the trees,
And felt the breath of the morning breeze
Blowing over the meadows brown.
And one was safe and asleep in his bed
Who at the bridge would be first to fall.
Who that day would be lying dead,
Pierced by a British musket ball.

You know the rest. In the books you have read
How the British Regulars fired and fled—

How the farmers gave them ball for ball,
From behind each fence and farmyard wall,
Chasing the red-coats down the lane,
Then crossing the fields to emerge again
Under the trees at the turn of the road,
And only pausing to fire and load.

So through the night rode Paul Revere;
And so through the night went his cry of alarm
To every Middlesex village and farm,
A cry of defiance and not of fear.
A voice in the darkness, and knock at the door,
And a word that shall echo for evermore!

For, borne on the night-wind of the Past,
Through all our history, to the last,
In the hour of darkness and peril and need,
The people will waken and listen to hear
The hurrying hoof-beats of that steed,
And the midnight message of Paul Revere.

HENRY WADSWORTH LONGFELLOW

KING CANUTE

King Canute was weary-hearted; he had reigned for years a score,
Battling, struggling, pushing, fighting, killing much and robbing
    more;
And he thought upon his actions, walking by the wild sea-shore.

'Twixt the chancellor and bishop walked the king with steps
    sedate,
Chamberlains and grooms came after, silversticks and gold-sticks
    great,
Chaplains, aides-de-camp, and pages, all the officers of state.
Sliding after like his shadow, pausing when he chose to pause;
If a frown his face contracted, straight the courtiers dropped
    their jaws;
If to laugh the king was minded, out they burst in loud hee-haws.

But that day a something vexed him, that was clear to old and
    young;
Thrice his grace had yawned at table, when his favourite gleemen
    sung,
Once the queen would have consoled him, but he bade her hold
    her tongue.

'Something ails my gracious master,' cried the Keeper of the Seal.
'Sure, my lord, it is the lampreys served at dinner, or the veal?'
'Pshaw!' exclaimed the angry monarch, 'Keeper, 'tis not that
    I feel.'
''Tis the heart and not the dinner, fool, that doth my rest impair:
Can a king be great as I am, prithee, and yet know no care?
Oh, I'm sick and tired, and weary.' —Some one cried, 'The
    King's arm-chair!'

Then towards the lackeys turning, quick my lord the Keeper nod-
    ded,
Straight the king's great chair was brought him, by two footmen
    able-bodied;

Languidly he sank into if; it was comfortably wadded.
'Leading on my fierce companions,' cried he, 'over storm and
    brine
I have fought and I have conquered! where was glory like to mine?'
Loudly all the courtiers echoed: 'Where is glory like to thine?'

'What avail me all my kingdoms? Weary am I now and old;
Those fair sons I have begotten, long to see me dead and cold;
Would I were, and quiet buried underneath the silent mould!'

'Nay, I feel,' replied King Canute, 'that my end is drawing near.
'Don't say so,' exclaimed the courtiers (striving each to squeeze
    a tear)
'Sure your grace is strong and lusty, and may live this fifty year,'

'Live these fifty years!' the bishop roared, with actions made to
    suit,

'Are you mad, my good Lord Keeper, thus to speak of King Canute!
Men have lived a thousand years, and sure his majesty will do't.'

'Did not once the Jewish captain stay the sun upon the hill,
And, the while he slew the foemen, bid the silver moon stand still?
So, no doubt, could gracious Canute, if it were his sacred will.'

'Might I stay the sun above us, good Sir Bishop?' Canute cried;'
'Could I bid the silver moon to pause upon her heavenly ride?
If the moon obeys my orders, sure I can command the tide'
'Will the advancing waves obey me, bishop, if I make the sign?'
Said the bishop, bowing lowly, 'Land and sea, my lord, are thine.'
Canute turned towards the ocean— 'Back!' he said, 'thou foaming
    brine!'

But the sullen ocean answered with a louder, deeper roar,
And the rapid waves drew nearer, falling sounding on the shore;
Back the keeper and the bishop, back the king and courtiers bore.

And he sternly bade them never more to kneel to human clay,
But alone to praise and worship that which earth and seas obey:
And his golden crown of empire never wore he from that day.

WILLIAM MAKEPEACE THACKERAY

KING PORUS—A LEGEND OF OLD

> *We never shall look upon his like again!*
>
> SHAKESPEARE
>
> *When shall such a hero live again?*
>
> BYRON

I

Loudly the midnight tempest sang,
Ah! it was thy dirge, fair Liberty!
And clouds in thundering accents roar'd
Unheeded warning from on high;
The rain in darksome torrents fell,
Hydaspes' waves did onward sweep,

Like fiery Passion's headlong flow,
To meet th' awaken'd calling deep;
The lightning flashed bright—dazzling, like
Fair woman's glance from 'neath her veil:
And on the heaving, troubled air,
There was a moaning sound of wail!
But, Ind! thy unsuspecting sons
Did heedless slumber,'—while the foe
Came in stealthy step of death,—
Came as the tiger, noiseless, slow,
To close at once its victim's breath!
Alas! they knew not 'midst this gloom,
This war of elements, was nurst,—
Like to an earthquake in the womb
Of a volcano,—deep and low—
A deadlier storm—on them to burst!

II

'Twas morn; the Lord of Day
From gold Sumero's palace bright,
Look'd on his own sweet clime,
But, lo! the glorious flag,
To which the world in awe once bow'd,
There in defiance waved
On India's gales—triumphant—proud!—
Then, rose the dreadful yell,—
Then lion-like, each warrior brave
Rushed on the coming foe,
To strike for freedom—or the grave!
Oh Death! upon thy gory altar
What blood-libations freely flow'd!
Oh Earth! on that bright morn, what thousands.
Rendered to thee the dust they ow'd!
But 'fore the Macedonians driven,
Fell India's hardy sons,—
Proud mountain oaks by thunders riven —
That for their country's freedom bled—
And made on gore their glorious bed!

III

But dauntlessly there stood
King Porus, towering 'midst the foe,
Like a Himala–peak
With its eternal crown of snow:
And on his brow did shine
The jewell'd regal diadem.
His milk-white elephant
Was deck'd with many a brilliant gem.
He reck'd not of the phalanx
That 'round him closed—but nobly fought,
And like the angry winds that blow
And lofty mountain pines lay low,
Amidst them dreadful havoc wrought,
And thinn'd his crown and country's foe!
The hardiest warriors, at his deeds,
Awe–struck quail'd like wind-shaken reeds:
They dared not look upon his face,
They shrank before his burning gaze,
For in his eye the hero shone
That feared not death;—but high—alone—
A being as if of lightning made,
That scorch'd all that is gazed upon—
Trampling the living with the dead.

IV

Th' immortal Thund'rer's son,
Astonish'd eyed the heroic king;
He saw him bravely charge
Like his dread father,—fulmining:—
Tho' thousands 'round him closed,
He stood—as stands the ocean rock
Amidst the lashing billows
Unmoved at their fierce thundering shock.
But when th' Emathian conqueror
Saw that with gaping wounds he bled,
'Desist—desist!'—he cried—
'Such noble blood should not be shed!'

Then a herald was sent
Where bleeding and faint,
Stood, 'midst the dying and the dead,
King Porus,—boldly, undismayed:
'Hail, brave and warlike prince!
Thy generous rival bids thee cease—
Behold! there flies the flag,
That lulls dread war, and wakens peace!'

V

Like to a lion chain'd.
That tho' faint—bleeding—stands in pride—
With eyes, where unsubdued
Yet flash'd the fire—looks that defied;
King Porus boldly went
Where 'midst the gay and flittering crowd
Sat god-like Alexander;
While 'round, Earth's mightiest monarchs bow'd.
King Porus was no slave;
He stooped not—bent not there his knee,—
But stood, as stands an oak,
In Himalayan majesty.
How should I treat thee?' ask'd
The mighty king of Macedon:
'Ev'n as a King,' replied
In royal pride, Ind's haughty son.
The conqu'ror pleas'd,
Him forth releas'd:
Thus India's crown was lost and won.

VI

But where, oh! where is Porus now?
And where the noble hearts that bled
For freedom—with the heroic glow
In patriot bosoms nourished—
—Hearts, eagle-like that recked not death,
But shrank before foul Thraldom's breath?
And where art thou—fair Freedom!—thou

Once goodness of Ind's sunny clime!
When glory's halo round her brow
Shone radiant, and she rose sublime,
Like her own towering Himalye
To kiss the blue clouds thron'd on high!
Clime of the sun!—how like a Dream—
How like bright sun-beams on a stream
That melt beneath gray twilight's eye—
That glory hath now flitted by!
The crown that once did deck thy brow
Is trampled down—and thou sunk low;
Thy pearl, thy diamond and thy mine
Of glistening gold no more is thine.
Alas!—each conquering tyrant's lust
Has robb'd thee of thy very dust!
Thou standest like a lofty tree
Shorn of fruits—blossoms—leaves and all—
Of every gale the sport to be.
Despised and scorned e'en in thy fall?

                    MICHAEL MADHUSUDAN DUTT

ULYSSES

It little profits that an idle king,
By this still hearth, among these barren crags,
Match'd with an aged wife, I mete and dole
Unequal laws unto a savage race,
That hoard, and sleep, and feed, and know not me.

    I cannot rest from travel: I will drink
Life to the lees: all times I have enjoy'd
Greatly, have suffer'd greatly, both with those
That loved me, and alone; on shore, and when
Thro' scudding drifts the rainy Hyades
Vext the dim sea: I am become a name;
For always roaming with a hungry heart
Much have I seen and known; cities of men
And manners, climates, councils, governments.

Myself not least, but honour'd of them all;
And drunk delight of battle with my peers,
Far on the ringing plains of windy Troy.

I am a part of all that I have met;
Yet all experience is an arch wherethro'
Gleams that untravell'd world, whose margin fades
For ever and for ever when I move.
How dull it is to pause, to make an end
To rust unburnish'd, not to shine in use!
As tho' to breathe were life. Life piled on life
Were all too little, and of one to me
Little remains: but every hour is saved
From that eternal silence, something more,
A bringer of new things; and vile it were
For some three suns to store and hoard myself,
And this grey spirit, yearning in desire
To follow knowledge, like a sinking star,
Beyond the utmost bound of human thought.

This is my son, mine own Telemachus,
To whom I leave the sceptre and the isle—
Well-loved of me, discerning to fulfil
This labour, by slow prudence to make mild
A rugged people and thro' soft degrees
Subdue them to the useful and the good.
Most blameless is he, centred in the sphere
Of common duties, decent not to fail
In offices of tenderness, and pay
Meet adoration to my household gods,
When I am gone. He works his work, I mine.

There lies the port: the vessel puffs her sail:
There gloom the dark broad seas. My mariners,
Souls that have toil'd, and wrought, and thought with me—
That ever with a frolic welcome took
The thunder and the sunshine, and opposed
Free hearts, free foreheads—you and I are old;

Old age hath yet his honour and his toil;
Death closes all: but something ere the end,
Some work of noble note, may yet be done,
Not unbecoming men that strove with Gods.
The lights begin to twinkle from the rocks:
The long day wanes: the slow moon climbs: the deep
Moans round with many voices. Come, my friends,
'Tis not too late to seek a newer world.
Push off, and, sitting well in order smite
The sounding furrows; for my purpose holds
To sail beyond the sunset, and the baths
Of all the western stars, until I die.
It may be that the gulfs will wash us down:
It may be we shall touch the Happy Isles,
And see the great Achilles, whom we knew.
Tho' much is taken, much abides; and tho'
We are not now that strength which in old days
Moved earth and heaven; that which we are, we are;
One equal temper of heroic hearts,
Made weak by time and fate, but strong in will
To strive, to seek, to find, and not to yield.

ALFRED, LORD TENNYSON

UPON WESTMINSTER BRIDGE
SEPTEMBER 3, 1802

Earth has not anything to show more fair:
Dull would he be of soul who could pass by
A sight so touching in its majesty:
This City now doth like a garment wear
The beauty of the morning; silent, bare,
Ships, towers, domes, theatres, and temples lie
Open unto the fields, and to the sky,—
All bright and glittering in the smokeless air.
Never did sun more beautifully steep
In his first splendour valley, rock, or hill;
Ne'er saw I, never felt, a calm so deep!
The river glideth at his own sweet will:

Dear God! the very houses seem asleep;
And all that mighty heart is lying still!

WILLIAM WORDSWORTH

SONNET ON CHILLON

Eternal Spirit of the chainless Mind!
Brightest in dungeons, Liberty, thou art—
For there thy habitation is the heart—
The heart which love of Thee alone can bind;
And when thy sons to fetters are consign'd,
To fetters, and the damp vault's dayless gloom,
Their country conquers with their martyrdom,
And Freedom's fame finds wings on every wind

Chillon! thy prison is a holy place
And thy sad floor an altar, for 'twas trod.
Until his very steps have left a trace

Worn as if thy cold pavement were a sod,
By Bonnivard! May none those marks efface'
For they appeal from tyranny to God.

GEORGE GORDON NOEL, LORD BYRON

10. SATIRE AND HUMOUR

JOHN GILPIN

John Gilpin was a citizen
    Of credit and renown,
A train-band captain eke was he
    Of famous London Town.

John Gilpin's spouse said to her dear—
    Thou wedded we have been
These twice ten tedious years, yet we
    No holiday have seen.

To-morrow is our wedding-day,
    And we will then repair
Unto the Bell at Edmonton
    All in a chaise and pair.

My sister, and my sister's child,
    Myself, and children three,
Will fill the chaise; so you must ride
    On horseback after we.

He soon replied—I do admire
    Of womankind but one,
And you are she, my dearest dear,
    Therefore it shall be done.

I am a linen-draper bold,
    As all the world doth know,
And my good friend the calender
    Will lend his horse to go.

Quoth Mrs. Gilpin— That's well said;
    And, for that wine is dear.

We will be furnish'd with our own,
    Which is both bright and clear.

John Gilpin kissed his loving wife;
    O'erjoyed was he to find
That, though on pleasure she was bent,
    She had a frugal mind.

The morning came, the chaise was brought,
    But yet was not allowed
To drive up to the door, lest all
    Should say that she was proud.

So three doors off the chaise was stayed,
    Where they did all get in;
Six precious souls, and all agog
    To dash through thick and thin!

Smack went the whip, round went the wheels,
    Were never folk so glad;
The stones did rattle underneath,
    As if Cheapside were mad.

John Gilpin, at his horse's side,
    Seized fast the flowing mane,
And up he got, in haste to ride.
    But soon came down again;

For saddle-tree scarce reached had he,
    His journey to begin,
When, turning round his head, he saw
    Three customers come in.

So down he came; for loss of time,
    Although it grieved him sore,
Yet loss of pence, full well he knew,
    Would trouble him much more.

'Twas long before the customers
   Were suited to their mind,
When Betty screaming came downstairs—
   The wine is left behind!

Good lack! quoth he—yet bring it me,
   My leathern belt likewise.
In which I bear my trusty sword
   When I do exercise.

Now mistress Gilpin (careful soul!)
   Had two stone bottles found,
To hold the liquor that she loved.
   And keep it safe and sound.

Each bottle had a curling ear.
   Through which the belt he drew.
And hung a bottle on each side.
   To make his balance true.

Then, over all. that he might be
   Equipped from top to toe,
His long red cloak, well brushed and neat,
   He manfully did throw.

Now see him mounted once again
   Upon his nimble steed,
Full slowly pacing o'er the stones.
   With caution and good heed!

But finding soon a smoother road
   Beneath his well-shod feet.
The snorting beast began to trot,
   Which galled him in his seat.

So, Fair and softly, John he cried,
   But John he cried in vain;
That trot became a gallop soon,
   In spite of curb and rein.

So stooping down, as needs he must
   Who cannot sit upright,
He grasped the mane with both his hands,
   And eke with all his might.

His horse, who never in that sort
   Had handled been before,
What thing upon his back had got
   Did wonder more and more.

Away went Gilpin, neck or nought;
   Away went hat and wig!—
He little dreamt, when he set out,
   Of running such a rig!

The wind did blow, the cloak did fly,
   Like streamer long and gay,
Till, loop and button failing both,
   At last it flew away.

Then might all people well discern
   The bottles he had slung;
A bottle swinging at each side,
   As hath been said or sung.

The dogs did bark, the children screamed,
   Up flew the windows all;
And every soul cried out—Well done!
   As loud as he could bawl.

Away went Gilpin—who but he?
   His fame soon spread around—
He carries weight! he rides a race!
   'Tis for a thousand pound!

And still, as fast as he drew near,
   'Twas wonderful to view
How in a trice the turnpike men
   Their gates wide open threw.

And now, as he went bowing down
   His reeking head full low,

The bottles twain behind his back
    Were shattered at a blow.

Down ran the wine into the road,
    Most piteous to be seen,
Which made his horse's flanks to smoke
    As they had basted been.

But still he seemed to carry weight,
    With leathern girdle braced;
For all might see the bottle-necks
    Still dangling at his waist.

Thus all through merry Islington
    These gambols he did play,
And till he came unto the Wash
    Of Edmonton so gay.

And there he threw the wash about
    On both sides of the way,
Just like unto a trundling mop.
    Or a wild goose at play.

At Edmonton his loving wife
    From the balcony spied
Her tender husband, wondering much
    To see how he did ride.

Stop, stop, John Gilpin!—Here's the house—
    They all at once did cry;
The dinner waits, and we are tired;
    Said Gilpin—So am I!

But yet his horse was not a whit
    Inclined to tarry there; For why?
his owner had a house
    Full ten miles off, at Ware.

So like an arrow swift he flew,

Shot by an archer strong;
So did he fly—which brings me to
   The middle of my song.

Away went Gilpin, out of breath,
   And sore against his will.
Till at his friend the calender's
   His horse at last stood still

The calender, amazed to see
   His neighbour in such trim.
Laid down his pipe, flew to the gate.
   And thus accosted him:—

What news? what news? your tidings tell;
   Tell me you must and shall—
Say why bare-headed you are come,
   Or why you come at all?

Now Gilpin had a pleasant wit,
   And loved a timely joke;
And thus unto the calender
   In merry guise he spoke:—

I came because your horse would come;
   And, if I well forebode,
My hat and wig will soon be here—
   They are upon the road.

The calender, right glad to find
   His friend in merry pin,
Returned him not a single word,
   But to the house went in;

Whence straight he came with hat and wig;
   A wig that flowed behind,
A hat not much the worse for wear,
   Each comely in its kind.

He held them up, and, in his turn,
    Thus showed his ready wit—
My head is twice as big as yours,
    They therefore needs must fit.

But let me scrape the dirt away,
    That hangs upon your face;
And stop and eat, for well you may
    Be in a hungry case.

Said John—It is my wedding-day,
    And all the world would stare,
If wife should dine at Edmonton
    And I should dine at Ware.

So, turning to his horse, he said—
    I am in haste to dine;
'Twas for your pleasure you came here.
    You shall go back for mine.

Ah, luckless speech, and bootless boast!
    For which he paid full dear;
For, while he spake, a braying ass
    Did sing most loud and clear;

Whereat his horse did snort, as he
    Had heard a lion roar,
And galloped off with all his might,
    As he had done before.

Away went Gilpin, and away
    Went Gilpin's hat and wig!
He lost them sooner than at first—
    For why?—they were too big!

Now, mistress Gilpin, when she saw
    Her husband posting down

Into the country far away,
    She pulled out half-a-crown;

And thus unto the youth she said,
    That drove them to the Bell—
This shall be yours when you bring back
    My husband safe and well.

The youth did ride, and soon did meet
    John coming back amain;
Whom in a trice he tried to stop,
    By catching at his rein;

But, not performing what he meant,
    And gladly would have done,
The frighted steed ne frighted more,
    And made him faster run.

Away went Gilpin, and away
    Went post-boy at his heels!—
The post-boy's horse right glad to miss
    The lumbering of the wheels.

Six gentlemen upon the road,
    Thus seeing Gilpin fly,
With post-boy scampering in the rear,
    They raised the hue and cry:

Stop thief!—stop thief!—a highwayman!
    Not one of them was mute;
And all and each that passed that way
    Did join in the pursuit.

And now the turnpike gates again
    Flew open in short space;
The toll-men thinking, as before,
    That Gilpin rode a race.

And so he did—and won it too!—
   For he got first to town;
Nor stopped till where he had got up
   He did again get down.

Now let us sing—Long live the king,
   And Gilpin long live he;
And, when he next doth ride abroad,
   May I be there to see!

WILLIAM COWPER

MISS GEE

Let me tell you a little story
   About Miss Edith Gee;
She lived in Clevedon Terrace
   At Number 83.

She'd a slight squint in her left eye,
   Her lips they were thin and small,
She had narrow sloping shoulders
   And she had no bust at all.

She'd a velvet hat with trimmings,
   And a dark grey serge costume,
She lived in Clevedon Terrace
   In a small bed-sitting room.

She'd a purple mac for wet days,
   A green umbrella too to take,
She'd a bicycle with shopping basket
   And a harsh back-pedal brake.

The Church of Saint Aloysius
   Was not so very far;
She did a lot of knitting,
   Knitting for that Church Bazaar.

Miss Gee looked up at the starlight
   And said, 'Does anyone care
That I live in Clevedon Terrace
   On one hundred pounds a year?'

She dreamed-a dream one evening
   That she was the Queen of France
And the Vicar of Saint Aloysius
   Asked Her Majesty to dance.

But a storm blew down the palace,
   She was biking through a field of corn,
And a bull with the face of the Vicar
   Was charging with lowered horn.

She could feel his hot breath behind her,
   He was going to overtake;
And the bicycle went slower and slower
   Because of that back-pedal brake.

Summer made the trees a picture,
   Winter made them a wreck;
She bicycled to the evening service
   With her clothes buttoned up to her neck.

She passed by the loving couples,
   She turned her head away,
She passed by the loving couples
   And they didn't ask her to stay.

Miss Gee sat down in the side-aisle,
   She heard the organ play;
And the choir it sang so sweetly
   At the ending of the day,

Miss Gee knelt down in the side-aisle,
   She knelt down on her knees;
'Lead me not into temptation

But make me a good girl, please.'

The days and nights went by her
    Like waves round a Cornish wreck;
She bicycled down to the doctor
    With her clothes buttoned up to her neck

She bicycled down to the doctor,
    And rang the surgery bell;
'O, doctor, I've a pain inside me,
    And I don't feel very well.'

Doctor Thomas looked her over,
    And then he looked some more;
Walked over to his wash-basin,
    Said, 'Why didn't you come before?'

Doctor Thomas sat over his dinner,
    Though his wife was waiting to ring,
Rolling his bread into pellets;
    Said, 'Cancer's a funny .thing.

'Nobody knows what the cause is,
    Though some pretend they do;
It's like some hidden assassin
    Waiting to strike at you.

'Childless women get it,
    And men when they retire;
It's as if there had to be some outlet
    For their foiled creative fire.'
His wife she rang for the servant,
    Said, 'Don't be so morbid, dear;'
He sard: I saw Miss Gee this evening
    And she's a goner, I fear.'

They took Miss Gee to the hospital,
    She lay there a total wreck,

Lay in the ward for women
    With the bedclothes right up to her neck.

They laid her on the table,
    The students began to laugh;
And Mr. Rose the surgeon
    He cut Miss Gee in half.

Mr. Rose he turned to his students,
    Said, 'Gentlemen, if you please,
We seldom see a sarcoma
    As far advanced as this.'

They took her off the table,
    They wheeled away Miss Gee
Down to another department
    Where they study Anatomy.

They hung her from the ceiling,
    Yes, they hung up Miss Gee;
And a couple of Oxford Groupers
    Carefully dissected her knee.

W.H. AUDEN

ZIMRI: THE DUKE OF BUCKINGHAM

A numerous host of dreaming Saints succeed,
Of the true old enthusiastic breed:
'Gainst form and order they their power employ,
Nothing to build and all things to destroy.
But far more numerous was the herd of such
Who think too little and who talk too much.,..
Such were the tools; but a whole Hydra more
Remains of sprouting heads too long to score.
    Some of their chiefs were Princes of the land;
In the first rank of these did Zimri stand,
A man so various that he seemed to be
Not one, but all mankind's epitome:

Stiff in opinions, always in the wrong,
Was everything by starts and nothing long;
But, in the course of one revolving moon,
Was chemist, fiddler, statesman, and buffoon;
Then all for women, painting, rhyming, drinking,
Besides ten thousand freaks that died in thinking.
Blest madman, who could every hour employ
With something new to wish or to enjoy!
Railing and praising were his usual themes,
And both, to show his judgement, in extremes:
So over-violent or over-civil
That every man with him was God or Devil.
In squandering wealth was his peculiar art;
Nothing went unrewarded but desert.
Beggared by fools, whom still he found too late,
He had his jest, and they had his estate.
He laughed himself from Court; then sought relief
By forming parties, but could ne'er be chief:
For, spite of him, the weight of business fell
On Absalom and wise Achitophel;
Thus wicked but in will, of means bereft,
He left not faction, but of that was left.

JOHN DRYDEN

MACAVITY: THE MYSTERY CAT

Macavity's a Mystery Cat: he's called the Hidden Paw—
For he's the master criminal who can defy the Law.
He's the bafflement of Scotland Yard, the Flying Squad's despair:
For when they reach the scene of crime:—Macavity's not there!
Macavity, Macavity, there's no one like Macavity,
He's broken every human law, he breaks the law of gravity.
His powers of levitation would make a fakir stare,
And when you reach the scene of crime—*Macavity's not there!*
You may seek him in the basement, you may look up in the air—
But I tell you once and once again, *Macavity's not there!*

Macavity's a ginger cat, he's very tall and thin;

You would know hint if you saw him, for his eyes are sunken in.
His brow is deeply lined with thought, his head is highly domed;
His coat is dusty from neglect, his whiskers are uncombed.
He sways his head from side to side, with movements like a snake;
And when you think he's half asleep, he's always wide awake.

Macavity, Macavity, there's no one like Macavity,
For he's a fiend in feline shape, a monster of depravity.
You may meet him in a by-street, you may see him in the square—
But when a crime's discovered, then *Macavity's not there!*

He's outwardly respectable. (They say be cheats at cards.)
And his footprints are not found in any file of Scotland Yard's.
And when the larder's looted, or the jewel-case is rifled,
Or when the milk is missing, or another Peke's been stifled,
Or the greenhouse glass is broken, and the trellis past repair—
Ay, there's the wonder of the thing! *Macavity's not there!*

And when the Foreign Office find a Treaty's gone astray,
Or the Admiralty lose some plans and drawings by the way,
There may be a scrap of paper in the hall or on the stair—
But it's useless to investigate—*Macavity's not there!*
And when the loss has been disclosed, the Secret Service say
'It *must* have been Macavity!' but he's a mile away.
You'll be sure to find him resting, or a-licking of his thumbs,
Or engaged in doing complicated long division sums.

Macavity, Macavity, there's no one like Macavity,
There never was a Cat of such deceitfulness and suavity.
He always has an alibi, and one or two to spare:
At whatever time the deed took place—MACAVITY WASN'T THERE!
And they say that all the Cats whose wicked deeds are widely
    known
(I might mention Mungojerrie, I might mention Griddlebone)
Are nothing more than agents for the Cat who all the time
Just controls their operations: the Napoleon of Crime!

                                                T.S. ELIOT

THE PROFESSOR

Remember me? I am Professor Sheth.
Once 1 taught you geography. Now
I am retired, though my health is good.
My wife died some years back.
By God's grace, all my children
Are well settled in life.
One is Sales Manager,
One is Bank Manager.
Both have cars.
Other also doing well, though not so well.
Every family must have black sheep.
Sarala and Tarala are married,
Their husbands are very nice boys.
You won't believe but I have eleven grandchildren.
How many issues you have? Three?
That is good. These are days of family planning.
I am not against. We have to change with times.
Whole world is changing. In India also
We are keeping up. Our progress is progressing.
Old values are going, new values are coming.
Everything is happening with leaps and bounds.
I am going out rarely, now and then
Only, this is price of old age
But my health is O.K. Usual aches and pains.
No diabetes, no blood pressure, no heart attack.
This is because of sound habits in youth.
How is your health keeping?
Nicely? I am happy for that.
This year 1 am sixty-nine
and hope to score century.
You were so thin, like stick,
Now you are man of weight and consequence.
That is good joke.
If you are coming again this side by chance,
Visit please my humble residence also.
I am living just on opposite house's backside.

                                              NLSSIM EZEKIEL

THE WALRUS AND THE CARPENTER

The sun was shining on the sea,
Shining with all his might:
He did his very best to make
The billows smooth and bright—
And this was odd, because it was
The middle of the night.

The moon was shining sulkily,
Because she thought the sun
Had got no business to be there
After the day was done—
"It's very rude of him," she said,
"To come and spoil the fun."

The sea was wet as wet could be,
The sands were dry as dry.
You could not see a cloud, because
No cloud was in the sky:
No birds were flying overhead—
There were no birds to fly.

The Walrus and the Carpenter
Were walking close at hand;
They wept like anything to see
Such quantities of sand:
"If this were only cleared away,"
They said, "it *would* be grand!"

"If seven maids with seven mops
Swept it for half a year,"
"Do you suppose," the Walrus said,
"That they could get it clear?"
"I doubt it," said the Carpenter,
And shed a bitter tear.
"O Oysters, come and walk with us!"
The Walrus did beseech.

"A pleasant walk, a pleasant talk,
Along the briny beach:
We cannot do with more than four,
To give a hand to each."

The eldest Oyster looked at him,
But never a word he said:
The eldest Oyster winked his eye,
And shook his heavy head—
Meaning to say he did not choose
To leave the oyster-bed.

But four young Oysters hurried up,
All eager for the treat:
Their coats were brushed, their faces washed
Their shoes were clean and neat—
And this was odd, because, you know,
They hadn't any feet.

Four other Oysters followed them,
And yet another four;
And thick and fast they came at last,
And more, and more, and more—
All hopping through the frothy waves,
And scrambling to the shore.

The Walrus and the Carpenter
Walked on a mile or so,
And then they rested on a rock
Conveniently low:
And all the little Oysters stood
And waited in a row.

"The time has come," the Walrus said,
"To talk of many things:
Of shoes—and ships—and sealing-wax—
Of cabbages—and kings—
And why the sea is boiling hot—
And whether pigs have wings."

"But wait a bit," the Oysters cried,
"Before we have our chat:
For some of us are out of breath,
And all of us are fat!"
"No hurry!" said the Carpenter.
They thanked him much for that.

"A loaf of bread," the Walrus said,
"Is what we chiefly need:
Pepper and vinegar besides
Are very good indeed—
Now if you're ready, Oysters dear,
We can begin to feed."

"But not on us!" the Oysters cried
Turning a little blue.
"After such kindness that would be
A dismal thing to do!"
"The night is fine," the Walrus said,
"Do you admire the view?"

"It was so kind of you to come:
And you are very nice!"
The Carpenter said nothing but,
"Cut us another slice:
I wish you were not quite so deaf—
I've had to ask you twice!"

"It seems a shame," the Walrus said,
"To play them such a trick,
After we've brought them out so far,
And made them trot so quick!"
The Carpenter said nothing but,
"The butter's spread too thick."

"I weep for you," the Walrus said,
"I deeply sympathize."

With sobs and tears he sorted out
Those of the largest size,
Holding his pocket-handkerchief
Before his streaming eyes.

"O Oysters," said the Carpenter,
"You've had a pleasant run!
Shall we be trotting home again?"
But answer there was none—
And this was scarcely odd, because
They'd eaten every one.

LEWIS CARROLL

MOSQUITO

When did you start your tricks
Monsieur?

What do you stand on such high legs for?
Why this length of shredded shank
You exaltation?

Is it so that you shall lift your centre of gravity upwards
And weigh no more than air as you alight upon me,
Stand upon me weightless, you phantom?

I heard a woman call you the Winged Victory
In sluggish Venice.
You turn your head towards your tail, and smile.

How can you put so much devilry
Into that translucent phantom shred
Of a frail corpus?

Queer, with your thin wings and your streaming legs
How you sail like a heron, on a dull clot of air,
A nothingness.

Yet what an aura surrounds you;
Your evil little aura, prowling, and casting a numbness on my
  mind.

That is your trick, your bit of filthy magic:
Invisibility, and the anaesthetic power
To deaden my attention in your direction.

But I know your game now, streaky sorcerer.

Queer, how you stalk and prowl the air
In circles and evasions, enveloping me,
Ghoul on wings
Winged Victory.

Settle, and stand on long thin shanks
Eyeing me sideways, and cunningly conscious that I am aware,
  You speck.

I hate the way you lurch off sideways into air
Having read my thoughts against you.

Come then, let us play at unawares,
And see who wins in this sly game of bluff,
Man or mosquito.

You don't know that I exist, and I don't know that you exist.
  Now then!

It is your trump
It is your hateful little trump
You pointed fiend,
Which shakes my sudden blood to hatred of you:
It is your small, high, hateful bugle in my ear.

Why do you do it?
Surely it is bad policy.

They say you can't help it.

If that is so, then I believe a little in Providence protecting the
    innocent.
But it sounds so amazingly like a slogan,
A yell of triumph as you snatch my scalp.

Blood, red blood
Super-magical
Forbidden liquor.

I behold you stand
For a second enspasmed-in oblivion,
Obscenely ecstasied
Sucking live blood,
My blood.

Such silence, such suspended transport,
Such gorging,
Such obscenity of trespass.

You stagger
As well as you may.
Only your accursed hairy frailty
Your own imponderable weightlessness
Saves you, wafts you away on the very draught my anger makes
    in its snatching.

Away with a paean of derision
You winged blood-drop.

Can I not overtake you?
Are you one too many for me,
Winged Victory?
Am I hot mosquito enough to out-mosquito you?

Queer, what a big stain my sucked blood makes
Beside the infinitesimal faint smear of you!
Queer, what a dim dark smudge you have disappeared into!

D.H. LAWRENCE

THE NOSE
(AFTER GOGOL)

The nose went away by itself
in the early morning
while its owner was asleep.
It walked along the road
sniffing at everything.

It thought: I have a personality of my own.
Why should I be attached to a body?
I haven't been allowed to flower.
So much of me has been wasted.

And it felt wholly free.
It almost began to dance
The world was so full of scents
it had had no time to notice,

when it was attached to a
face weeping, being blown,
catching all sorts of germs
and changing colour.

But now it was quite at ease
bowling merrily along
like a hoop or a wheel,
a factory packed with scent.

And all would have been well
but that, round about evening,

having no eyes for guides,
it staggered into the path

of a mouth, and it was gobbled
rapidly like a sausage
and chewed by great sour teeth—
and that was how it died.

IAN CRICHTON SMITH

CULTURE

Bred among odours of ordure
I missed the chance to nose
A pure damask rose.
Now fully grown I realize
We were only taught to use
Green fields as lavatories,
And therefore I have come to associate
All kinds of hues
Merely with animal or human waste.
A tinge of minivet-scarlet
Is no reminiscence of that bird.
But of betel-spittle stains
Left by movie fans
On walls of cinema halls,
And by pimps and harlots
In red-light lanes.

Siris leaves possess
An autumn flavescence immeasurably less
Than expectorations of asthmatic old men
Coughing doubled-up on loose
Squeaky string cots whose
Rans of twine
Are bro—
Ken as their thoughts.

A takin-gold evokes
Not in the least
Memories of dawn or some rare beast,
But scats of stray dogs
Like pagoda heaps
Among scattered slippers
Of scores of worshippers
At a Vashnoi temple-feast.

Tourists note
Fresco-amber
In Ajanta art.
I know this pigment from
Pools of bovine piss
At any vegetable mart.

ASHOK MAHAJAN